Kant's *Religion within the Boundaries of Mere Reason*

READER'S GUIDES

Bloomsbury *Reader's Guides* are clear, concise and accessible introductions to key texts in literature and philosophy. Each book explores the themes, context, criticism and influence of key works, providing a practical introduction to close reading, guiding students towards a thorough understanding of the text. They provide an essential, up-to-date resource, ideal for undergraduate students.

Titles available in this series:

Aristotle's *Metaphysics*, Edward Halper
Aristotle's *Politics*, Judith A. Swanson and C. David Corbin
Badiou's *Being and Event*, Christopher Norris
Berkeley's *Principles of Human Knowledge*, Alasdair Richmond
Berkeley's *Three Dialogues*, Aaron Garrett
Deleuze and Guattari's *A Thousand Plateaus*, Eugene W. Holland
Deleuze and Guattari's *What is Philosophy?*, Rex Butler
Deleuze's *Difference and Repetition*, Joe Hughes
Derrida's *Writing and Difference*, Sarah Wood
Hegel's *Phenomenology of Spirit*, Stephen Houlgate
Heidegger's *Later Writings*, Lee Braver
Hume's *Enquiry Concerning Human Understanding*, Alan Bailey and Dan O'Brien
Kant's *Critique of Aesthetic Judgement*, Fiona Hughes
Kierkegaard's *Fear and Trembling*, Clare Carlisle
Kuhn's *The Structure of Scientific Revolutions*, John Preston
Locke's *Essay Concerning Human Understanding*, William Uzgalis
Mill's *Utilitarianism*, Henry R. West
Machiavelli's *The Prince*, Miguel Vatter
Nietzsche's *Beyond Good and Evil*, Christa Davis Acampora and Keith Ansell Pearson
Nietzsche's *The Birth of Tragedy*, Douglas Burnham and Martin Jesinghausen
Nietzsche's *Thus Spoke Zarathustra*, Clancy Martin and Daw-Nay Evans
Plato's *Republic*, Luke Purshouse

Plato's *Symposium*, Thomas L. Cooksey
Rawls's *A Theory of Justice*, Frank Lovett
Sartre's *Being and Nothingness*, Sebastian Gardner
Schopenhauer's *The World as Will and Representation*, Robert L. Wicks
Wittgenstein's *Philosophical Investigations*, Arif Ahmed

A READER'S GUIDE

Kant's *Religion within the Boundaries of Mere Reason*

EDDIS N. MILLER

BLOOMSBURY
LONDON • NEW DELHI • NEW YORK • SYDNEY

Bloomsbury Academic
An imprint of Bloomsbury Publishing Plc

50 Bedford Square	1385 Broadway
London	New York
WC1B 3DP	NY 10018
UK	USA

www.bloomsbury.com

Bloomsbury is a registered trade mark of Bloomsbury Publishing Plc

First published 2015

© Eddis N. Miller, 2015

Eddis N. Miller has asserted his right under the Copyright, Designs and Patents Act, 1988, to be identified as Author of this work.

Text extracts taken from Immanuel Kant, edited and translated by Allen Wood, George Di Giovanni, *Kant: Religion within the Boundaries of Mere Reason: And Other Writings*, 1998 © Cambridge University Press, reproduced with permission.

All rights reserved. No part of this publication may be reproduced or transmitted in any form or by any means, electronic or mechanical, including photocopying, recording, or any information storage or retrieval system, without prior permission in writing from the publishers.

No responsibility for loss caused to any individual or organization acting on or refraining from action as a result of the material in this publication can be accepted by Bloomsbury Academic or the author.

British Library Cataloguing-in-Publication Data
A catalogue record for this book is available from the British Library.

ISBN: HB: 978-1-47251-410-3
PB: 978-1-47250-770-9
ePDF: 978-1-47250-944-4
ePub: 978-1-47250-763-1

Library of Congress Cataloging-in-Publication Data
A catalog record for this book is available from the Library of Congress.

Typeset by Deanta Global Publishing Services, Chennai, India

TABLE OF CONTENTS

Preface ix

1 Context 1
2 Overview of themes 9
3 Reading the text 13
   Prefaces to the first and second editions 13
   Part I of the *Religion* 19
   Part II of the *Religion* 60
   Part III of the *Religion* 84
   Part IV of the *Religion* 114
4 Reception and influence 133
5 Guide for further reading 141

Bibliography 145
Index 151

PREFACE

This book is one among a number of guides and commentaries to Kant's *Religion within the Boundaries of Mere Reason* that have appeared or will be appearing within a very short time span, testifying to a resurgence of scholarly interest in this text. Given this wealth of new secondary literature, I would like, at the outset, to make some remarks concerning the intentions and approach of this particular book.

This book is not a comprehensive commentary on the *Religion*. It is a "reader's guide," a distinct genre of text, targeted at an advanced undergraduate audience. While I hope to have said plenty that is of interest to the Kant scholar, I have tried my best not to abdicate my duty to this audience. Therefore, the reader should bear in mind a number of points. First, I have made every effort not to entangle the reader in the ever-growing body of secondary scholarship on the *Religion*. There is a "Guide for Further Reading" at the end of the book that will suggest some places to begin for students who are interested in investigating the *Religion* beyond this reader's guide. Second, Kant's *Religion* is a very complex text; it was neither possible, given space limitations, nor advisable, given the intended audience, to comment on every detail. I am confident, however, that those parts of the text that had to be passed over quickly or in silence are not crucial for an understanding of the main themes, concepts, and strategies of the *Religion*. Third, a comprehensive commentary would require that the *Religion* be thoroughly situated within Kant's larger corpus. In general, I have tried to engage Kant's other texts as selectively as possible, and only where I felt it was absolutely necessary for the reader to understand the main arguments of the text. I have made every effort not to assume prior knowledge of Kant's other writings, though I anticipate that the *Religion* will typically not be the advanced philosophy major's first point of contact with Kant. Finally, Chapter 3 ("Reading the Text") begins with Kant's two prefaces and then proceeds through the four parts of the *Religion* (with their appended "General Remarks") in order. There are places, however, where I have taken the liberty of not strictly adhering to the order of Kant's exposition, most notably in my discussion of Part I. I have only done this where I felt that a different order of exposition would be most helpful to the reader. It should go without saying that this book is intended to be read *alongside* the *Religion*, not *in place of it*.

Several different English translations of Kant's *Religion* are in print. For the purposes of this book, I have made use of George di Giovanni's translation, which is printed in the volume of the Cambridge Edition of the Works of Immanuel Kant entitled *Religion and Rational Theology* (Cambridge University Press, 1996). This same translation is also published separately as part of the series "Cambridge Texts in the History of Philosophy" (Cambridge University Press, 1998). I thank Cambridge for giving me permission to quote from this translation. I have given all references to Kant's texts according to the Prussian Academy Edition pagination, with the sole exception of references to Kant's "Idea for a Universal History with a Cosmopolitan Aim," for which I have given the page number of the translation that I have used.

I would like to thank the editors and staff at Bloomsbury for their support and hard work. I owe a debt of gratitude to Caitlin Boley, one of my students at Pace University, who ably served as my "ideal reader," providing much valuable feedback. My endless gratitude goes to my family for their love and encouragement as I've written this book. My wife, Lisa Anderson, tirelessly read drafts of this book in all of its stages, some of them quite ugly, and bore with me graciously through the darker phases of book writing. Much of what is good and none of what is bad in this book is due to her.

CHAPTER ONE

Context

The writings of the German philosopher Immanuel Kant (1724–1804) have exerted a decisive and lasting influence in virtually every domain of philosophy, including the domain with which we will be primarily concerned in this book: the philosophy of religion. Kant's *Religion within the Boundaries of Mere Reason* (1793) stands as one of the greatest philosophical engagements with religion produced during the Enlightenment. While the *Religion* filters the Enlightenment approach to religion through a distinctly Kantian lens, it is very much a product of its time and has much in common with other writings on religion produced during the Enlightenment—or perhaps more accurately, during the various "Enlightenments" of the eighteenth century: the English and Scottish Enlightenment, the French *Lumières*, and the German *Aufklärung*.

One way to understand philosophical treatments of religion during the Enlightenment is as a response to problems of religious intolerance and violence in the wake of the Protestant Reformation. The so-called Wars of Religion of the sixteenth and seventeenth centuries led to widespread death and destruction throughout Europe. What is remarkable about this violence is that it was not violence between different religions but violence between groups that all claimed to be Christian—Catholics against Protestants, and one Protestant sect against another. Of course, the parties to these disputes often refused to recognize the Christian credentials of their opponents, but they nevertheless appealed to one and the same sacred text and to one and the same sacred history as the sources of their beliefs. One helpful way to view the treatment of religion by various Enlightenment philosophers is as an expression of weariness with this dogmatism, intolerance, and disunity, all of which seemed to them fundamentally *irrational*. To overcome these ills, many Enlightenment philosophers reconceived religion altogether through the lens of *reason* rather than *revelation*. Revelation—in this case, the Bible—could not provide the basis for adjudicating these disputes, seeing that the very same verses could be used to defend quite different positions; in short, revelation requires *interpretation*, and without any ground rules for interpretation, there seemed to be little hope for reconciliation.

If revelation could not provide the basis for adjudicating differences in matters of religion, reason seemed to hold out significantly more hope. For many Enlightenment thinkers, reason was perfectly sufficient to produce religion: the existence of God and his attributes could be known through reason; and if we assume that God is a moral God, then it is reasonable to expect that what he requires from humans is moral behavior. Since morality can be known through reason as well, no revelation is required to teach us what is right and what is wrong. Thus, reason can produce religion without the input of revelation, and all human beings can accept this stripped-down, rational religion, because all human beings are rational. As long as humans stay within the bounds of rational religion, the dissension, persecution, and violence that seem to go hand in hand with revealed religion can be overcome.

This, of course, is a very general characterization of Enlightenment religious ideas; in point of fact, there is no single "Enlightenment" view of religion. While a healthy optimism in the power of reason and a shared commitment to tolerance and freedom of thought form a common denominator, attitudes toward revelation and institutional religion varied greatly. For some, revelation—and perhaps even the existence of God—was to be rejected altogether as irrational and superstitious; for others, revelation was accepted to the extent that it could be shown to agree with reason; and for others still, revelation had an indispensable role to play in the "education" of humanity, though this role was thought to be coming to an end in an age of maturity and enlightenment. For some, institutional religion—and with it, the clergy—was corrupt and manipulative, to be done away with altogether; for others, religious institutions were capable of much good and perhaps even indispensable, provided that they worked in the service of rational religion.

Kant's *Religion*, as we will see, demonstrates a commitment to many of these ideas: it prioritizes reason, and particularly moral reason, over what Kant perceived to be blind, servile faith, dogmatism, and superstition; it attacks the "priestcraft" and spiritual despotism of religious authorities; it argues for morality as the key to the proper interpretation of scripture; it makes a powerful plea on behalf of tolerance and freedom of conscience in matters of religion; and while not altogether rejecting historical religion with its various institutions, scriptures, dogmas, and practices, it nevertheless locates the value of historical religion strictly in its function as a vehicle for the promotion of pure rational religion—a pure rational religion that will ultimately render such historical religion superfluous.

Prior to the publication of the *Religion*, Kant's writings on religion were not concerned with historical religion as such, but with a "pure religion of reason." For Kant, this pure religion of reason was a moral religion, an "ethicotheology" generated by reason in its practical capacity. The articulation of this ethicotheology required Kant first to clear away the detritus of traditional philosophical investigations into the existence and nature of God.

It is an old and enduring idea of Western philosophy and theology that God's existence can be proven through one or more rational arguments. In the *Critique of Pure Reason* (1781), Kant believed himself to have demonstrated once and for all the failure of any such proofs of God's existence. This failure results not simply from problems specific to the individual arguments for God's existence, though Kant did indeed point out some of their shortcomings. More profoundly, Kant attempted to demonstrate in the first *Critique* that humans could have no knowledge of the existence or inexistence of *supersensible* objects, that is, objects of which they can have no empirical intuition. And since God is, by definition, supersensible, humans cannot prove—or for that matter disprove—the existence of God, nor have any knowledge concerning the truth or falsity of propositions concerning matters transcendent and supernatural.

In rejecting this long-standing tradition of philosophical proofs of God's existence, Kant saw himself not as undermining belief in God's existence—the atheist who dogmatically denies God's existence transgresses the limits of human knowledge just as readily as the theist who dogmatically claims to know with incontrovertible certainty that God exists—but as opening the way for *faith*. After all, where there is knowledge, faith is superfluous if not impossible.

Kant says as much in the Preface to the second edition of the first *Critique*, when he writes that he had to "deny **knowledge** in order to make room for **faith**" (B xxx).

But the kind of faith whose path the first *Critique* clears is not a blind faith in the sacred texts, creeds, or dogmas of any historical religion, nor is it some divinely inspired and supernatural faith; rather, it is a faith generated by human practical (moral) reason. In its most basic terms, this moral faith, for Kant, arises from the fact that humans are both *rational* and *sensible* beings. As rational beings, humans bind themselves to a moral law that commands unconditionally. As sensible beings, however, they experience natural desires and inclinations that often come into conflict with the moral law. These natural inclinations are not evil in themselves, but when the human being freely subordinates the moral law to the satisfaction of his inclinations (self-love), he becomes evil. Does the moral law, then, require that the human being sacrifice his happiness (as the satisfaction of his inclinations) in its name? Yes, the moral law does demand such sacrifice, but since the human being is a sensible being, he can never altogether renounce an interest in his own happiness. So, rather than rejecting the moral law in the name of happiness, or renouncing happiness for the sake of the moral law, the human being asks himself what kind of happiness his moral reason can endorse. The happiness that his reason can approve of is not one that comes through violation of the moral law (even if this should prove to be the most expedient way to satisfy his natural inclinations); rather, it is a happiness that is proportioned to his *moral worthiness* of happiness, that is, happiness strictly proportioned to *virtue*. Kant calls happiness proportioned to virtue the "highest good," which is the rationally endorsed final end of humanity. The problem, however, is that virtue seems only unreliably to result in happiness in this world; so, the human being is led to the idea of a supremely powerful *moral* ruler of the world who is capable of uniting virtue and happiness. Thus, God, as a postulate of practical reason, becomes the object of the moral faith of humanity, a faith that gives strength to the human moral vocation. Religion—a moral and therefore rational religion—consists in nothing other than recognizing one's moral duties as being at the same time the commands of a moral God.

This moral, rational religion, articulated in the first *Critique* and further elaborated in the second and third *Critiques*—the

Critique of Practical Reason (1788) and the *Critique of the Power of Judgment* (1790)—depends in no way upon historical religious traditions (or so Kant believes); it is generated by practical reason without the intervention of scripture or tradition. Moral religion is an entirely philosophical enterprise. In *Religion within the Boundaries of Mere Reason* (1793), however, Kant went beyond this strictly philosophical analysis of religion and into the realm of historical religion. This extension of the reach of philosophy into the realm of historical religion came, as we will see, with serious consequences for Kant.

Frederick II, known as Frederick the Great, ruled Prussia from 1740 to 1786. His reign overlapped with the publication of some of Kant's most important texts, including the *Critique of Pure Reason* and the *Groundwork for the Metaphysics of Morals* (1785). Frederick was considered an exemplar of "enlightened absolutism" and would certainly have been sympathetic to the arguments of the *Religion* had he lived to read it: he shared with many of the Enlightenment thinkers an anticlerical and antidogmatic frame of mind and allowed freedom of thought in religious matters. Yet, his successor and nephew Frederick William II was devoutly—some might say fanatically—religious. He surrounded himself with a number of ultraconservative advisors, many of whom were Rosicrucians— members of a secret, esoteric society founded in late medieval Germany and associated with Lutheranism. The Rosicrucians were avowedly anti-Enlightenment. The most important of these figures for our purposes is Johann Christoph Wöllner, a Lutheran minister appointed as minister of culture under Frederick William II.

From his position as minister of culture, Wöllner issued the "Edict on Religion of 9 August 1788," designed to restrain the public discussion of religion and impose uniformity of doctrine on all texts used for study in the schools and universities. In the September of 1791, Kant published "On the Miscarriage of All Philosophical Trials in Theodicy," which obliquely, though unmistakably, spoke out against the policies of Frederick William II. This no doubt caught Wöllner's attention.

In the February of 1792, Kant sent an essay entitled "On Radical Evil in Human Nature" (the essay that would eventually become Part I of the *Religion*) to Johann Erich Biester, editor of the *Berlinische Monatsschrift*—one of the most important publications espousing Enlightenment views in Germany. Kant asked Biester to submit the essay to the censors in Berlin, even though this was not, in fact, necessary: due to opposition from Wöllner, this publication had actually been moved outside of Prussia to Jena and therefore did not fall under the jurisdiction of the Berlin censors. Nevertheless, Kant did not wish to give the appearance of avoiding the Berlin censors. The essay passed and appeared in the April of 1792.

Later that year, Kant sent Biester a second essay, entitled "Of the Struggle of the Good Principle with the Evil Principle for Sovereignty over Man." This time, the Berlin censors rejected Kant's essay. Whereas the first essay was thought to be philosophical and therefore of no danger to the public, this second essay seemed to the censors more overtly theological. Biester appealed the decision, but to no avail. Kant asked Biester to return the essay to him, and combining this essay with the previous one on radical evil as well as with two additional essays, Kant created *Religion within the Boundaries of Mere Reason*. Clearly, he would not have success if he sent this volume to the Berlin censors, but there was another option. Professors in Prussia had the right to have their work censored by the deans of their faculty. So, Kant sent the book to the faculty of theology at the University of Halle, who declared the book to be philosophical rather than theological: this meant that the faculty of philosophy could then decide whether to publish the book. Kant then sent it to the philosophy faculty in Jena, where it was approved and published in time for the Easter Book Fair in Leipzig in 1794.

Kant had, then, published a book part of which had been rejected by the Berlin censors, an act that, as Manfred Kuehn notes, could only be taken as a "slap in the face of Wöllner and his censors" (365). As a result, in the October of 1794, Wöllner wrote the following to Kant, at the order of the king:

> Our most high person has observed with great displeasure how you misuse your philosophy to distort and negatively evaluate many of the cardinal and basic teachings of the Holy Scripture and of Christianity; how you have done this particularly in your book *Religion within the Boundaries of Mere Reason*, as well as in shorter treatises. We expected better things of you as you yourself must realize, how irresponsibly you have acted against your duty as a teacher of the youth against our paternal purpose, which you know very well. We demand that you give at once a most conscientious account of yourself, and expect that in the

future, to avoid our highest disfavor, you will be guilty of no such fault.... Failing this, you must expect unpleasant measures for your continued obstinacy. (Quoted in Kuehn, 379)

The consequences for the then 70-year-old Kant might have included dismissal or forced retirement without pension from his university position, and perhaps even banishment. Kant responded to the king in a letter dated 12 October, defending himself against the king's charges, yet in the end issuing the following promise: "I believe the surest way, which will obviate the least suspicion, is for me to declare solemnly, as *Your majesty's loyal subject*, that I will hereafter refrain altogether from discoursing publicly, in lectures or writings, on religion, whether natural or revealed" (Quoted in Kuehn, 380).

By declaring that he would refrain from publishing on religion as his "majesty's loyal subject," Kant seemed to be leaving the door open to publish on religion should the king die before him. Indeed, after the king died in 1797, Kant published *The Conflict of the Faculties* (1798), part of which had been sitting ready in his desk since 1794. In this text, one finds a lengthy defense of the independence of the philosophy faculty from both the theology faculty and government censorship, even when investigating historical religion from a philosophical perspective. In addition, the *Conflict* outlines the hermeneutic principles with which the moral philosopher should interpret scripture—principles employed extensively throughout the *Religion*. The *Conflict* is, thus, a helpful source for understanding Kant's project in the *Religion*; we will briefly consider it in our discussion of Kant's two Prefaces to the *Religion* in Chapter 3.

CHAPTER TWO

Overview of themes

As we discussed in Chapter 1, Kant develops, in his three *Critiques*, the idea of a purely rational (moral) religion—a religion that can be known through reason alone and therefore does not depend upon historical revelations, traditions, dogmas, or practices. The *Religion*, by contrast, engages directly with historical religion. In the Preface to the second edition of the *Religion*, Kant says that the project of analyzing religion "within the boundaries of mere reason" consists in holding fragments of historical revelation up to moral concepts to see whether there is compatibility and unity between historical revelation and the religion of reason. Kant will indeed find such compatibility between rational religion and what he takes to be the heart of Christian revelation. And yet, there are many elements of historical religion that are not simply nonmoral, but actively work against morality. So, the task of the *Religion*, beyond the mere demonstration of unity between historical revelation and rational religion, will be to neutralize elements of Christianity that run counter to morality through a *moral interpretation* of Christian scripture, dogma, and practice. Kant will practice such moral exegesis of Christian revelation throughout the *Religion*.

The first element of Christian revelation that is subject to moral reinterpretation is the doctrine of original sin. The argument of Part I of the *Religion* is at once deeply pessimistic and profoundly optimistic. On the one hand, Kant asserts that human beings are radically evil and therefore stand in need of a total revolution of moral disposition; to this extent, Kant endorses the doctrine of original sin. (Understanding what precisely Kant means by radical evil, and why he ascribes this evil to humanity as a whole, will be one of our main tasks.) On the other hand, Kant insists that this evil is *freely chosen* by each human being—there can be no good or evil in a moral sense where there is no freedom—and therefore it is not present in the human being simply by virtue of his having been born a human being; in this respect, Kant rejects the basic premises of the doctrine of original sin. This is the basis for Kant's optimism: just as evil is freely chosen, so it can be freely rejected. For despite having chosen evil, there is in human beings an inextirpable predisposition to the good; humans experience the call of the moral law—a call to subordinate self-love and the satisfaction of one's own inclinations and desires to universal moral principles—and are able to freely respond to this call and bring about a moral revolution.

Part I, then, sets up the problem—radical evil—and Parts II and III address how this problem is to be overcome. For many Christian theologians—Luther included—humans are powerless to extricate themselves from the hold of original sin, and they depend entirely upon God's grace to heal this sinful nature and make them righteous; and the debt of sin that humanity bears on account of this original sin is only paid for through the atoning power of the crucifixion of Jesus Christ. Without divine grace, and without Christ paying the debt of sin on our behalf, humans would remain objects of divine displeasure, laden with infinite guilt and deserving of infinite punishment. Kant, as we will see, will not reject the Christian language of grace and atonement altogether; he will preserve it, but—just as he does with the doctrine of original sin—he will radically redefine it in order to bring it in line with morality. In Part II, Kant will interpret Jesus as a "prototype" of human moral perfection given sensible, narrative representation in scripture. While human reason generates this prototype on its own and to this extent does not *need* scriptural representation, Kant insists that on account of the weakness of finite human nature, humans demand sensible representations for moral concepts. Therefore, even though reason, strictly speaking, does not require sensible representations, historical revelation can play an important role in the moral progress of human beings—provided, however, that this revelation is interpreted in accordance with moral concepts.

The problem with the Christian doctrines of grace and atonement is that they put human beings in a position of passively awaiting and passively receiving their moral regeneration—this is unacceptable for Kant. A simple principle governs Kant's *Religion*: moral action is the only thing that one can do to become pleasing to God and actions are moral only when they originate in the free will of the human being who is performing them. Humans, therefore, must actively earn their own salvation by doing everything within their power to make themselves into the moral beings they ought to be. Kant will insist repeatedly that humans cannot have any knowledge of what, if anything, God contributes to the process of moral regeneration—and insofar as God is a supernatural being, humans are not capable of attaining any such knowledge. All that human beings can know and need to know is what they themselves must do in order to become worthy of divine assistance—and this can only be moral action. There are problems that arise, however, for the human being attempting to conform to the prototype of moral perfection. For example, even if the human being can freely choose to live morally, he cannot undo his past evil. How can he become pleasing to God in light of this unpaid debt of sin? In Part II, Kant will address this and other problems, and in so doing, creatively reinterpret the Christian doctrine of the atonement to bring it in line with moral concepts.

For Kant, the moral regeneration of the human being is not simply an individual affair. In the beginning of Part III, he argues that humans have a tendency to corrupt one another and therefore that evil cannot be eradicated unless humans work together to build an ethical community to combat this corrupting tendency. Just as Kant interprets Jesus as the prototype of human moral perfection, he interprets the "church" as the prototype of this ethical community. The true church, for Kant, is one that, while not yet purely rational, nevertheless serves as a vehicle for the promotion of pure rational religion; all of the historical and nonmoral elements of the historical church only find their meaning and value to the extent that they further this end. The history of moral religion begins when a historical church or ecclesiastical faith appears in the world that promotes pure moral religion. For Kant, the first such ecclesiastical faith, and therefore the first claimant to the title of "true church," is the Christian faith. He will attempt to substantiate his claim that Christianity is a moral religion through an analysis of Jesus' teachings, particularly those found in the Sermon on the Mount. But given the nonmoral elements present in any ecclesiastical faith, even Christianity, the only way for ecclesiastical faith to act as a vehicle for pure rational religion is through the moral interpretation of the scriptures, dogmas, and practices of that faith. Part III, therefore, makes the argument for the rights of the moral interpreter of revelation over and against rival claimants.

A central tension throughout the *Religion* arises from the peculiar relationship between historical faith and pure rational religion. On the one hand, Kant believes that historical faith serves as a vehicle for the promotion of pure moral religion; given the weakness of human nature, this vehicle is a necessary one, even if it will one day be dispensable. On the other hand, historical faith constantly threatens to undermine moral faith by substituting moral service of God with nonmoral service. Indeed, humans will go to great lengths to avoid the difficult work of moral improvement and therefore have a tendency to conceive of God as a being who is susceptible to flattery and for whom devotion can be demonstrated by arbitrary forms of service. In Part IV, Kant will analyze this human tendency to "religious delusion," "fetishism," and "counterfeit service" of God. Throughout the *Religion*, and in Part IV specifically, we find an impassioned plea for religious tolerance and freedom of conscience in religious matters. This plea is grounded both in Kant's claim that we can never have knowledge concerning the truth of the transcendent doctrines of revealed religion and in the conviction that these doctrines are ultimately secondary to true religious devotion, which consists in moral action alone.

CHAPTER THREE

Reading the text

Prefaces to the first and second editions

The *Religion* has two Prefaces, one to the first edition (1793) and one to the second (1794). We will focus on two of the main objectives of these prefaces: first, to give an account of how morality leads to religion and second, to explain the basic project of the *Religion*.

Morality and religion (6:3–6)

In the opening sentence of the first Preface, Kant emphatically states that morality has no need of the idea of God; the human being, Kant says, is a free being who binds himself through reason to unconditional moral laws—that is, laws that command what *must be done* regardless of the outcome. (The unconditional or *categorical* commands of the moral law contrast with conditional or *hypothetical* commands, which tell us what to do only if we want to obtain a particular result.) The human being does not need the idea of God in order to make clear to him what his duties are—he knows his duties through his own reason—nor does he need an incentive to follow his duty; he is capable of acting purely out of respect for the moral law. Morality, thus, has no need of God or religion. Yet, just a couple of pages later, Kant writes that morality inevitably leads to religion, thereby extending itself to the idea of a "mighty moral lawgiver" outside of the human being. How does Kant get from the independence and self-subsistence of morality to the ideas of God and religion? And how can morality truly be independent of religion if it leads inevitably to it?

In the intervening pages, Kant gives a very compressed argument for the connection between morality and religion. Kant is in effect repeating the results of his earlier investigations into rational religion in the first three *Critiques*. The reader who is unfamiliar with these texts will likely find Kant's brief, prefatory summation of these arguments rather bewildering. Our task, then, is to clarify the connection between morality and religion.

The cornerstone of Kant's ethical thought is the idea that there is only one way for an action to qualify as "moral": it must be done *out of respect for the moral law*. If the primary incentive to action (or what Kant calls the "sufficient determining ground") is anything other than respect for the moral law, then one's action may be *legal*—in mere *conformity* to the law—but not *moral*. Thus, when it comes to doing our duty, we should not look around for other incentives to motivate our actions. This is what it means to say that the moral law places an *unconditional* demand upon us: it obligates us to act in a certain way independently of the ends to be attained through that action.

If humans were purely rational beings, this would be the end of the story—the moral law would determine their will directly. But humans are not, according to Kant, purely rational beings: they are also *sensible* beings with natural inclinations, which they inevitably seek to satisfy. In a footnote, Kant defines "inclination" as the desire to possess a certain thing—or an "end"—through one's action (6:6n). The "final end" of the human being—the condition of all our other ends—is *happiness*.

It is worth reflecting, for a moment, on the difference between human beings and nonhuman animals. For Kant, humans share a sensible nature with nonhuman animals and are, therefore, subject to natural inclinations. Of course, the actions of nonhuman animals are determined directly by these inclinations, whereas humans are capable of deferring the immediate satisfaction of their inclinations in order to satisfy more distant ends. Nevertheless, insofar as both are sensible beings, they both experience natural inclinations. But the human being, unlike non-nonhuman animals, is also susceptible to the call of the moral law; in other words, humans have a moral predisposition that obligates them to renounce the satisfaction of their inclinations when these inclinations come into conflict with the unconditional demands of the moral law. The human being is a free being and therefore not immediately compelled to act according to nature's dictates.

The fact that the human being has a sensible nature means that even though the moral law commands unconditionally, the question will always insinuate itself for human reason: What will be the result of our good conduct? It seems obvious that moral action does not directly lead to the satisfaction of our inclinations (happiness). If satisfying inclinations were our primary goal, we would do much better to violate the moral law. But since the law commands unconditionally, we cannot simply set it aside when it is not an expedient means to the satisfaction of our inclinations. Rather, the only kind of happiness that a rational being who feels bound by the moral law can endorse is the idea of a happiness that follows upon his worthiness to be happy (virtue) and is directly proportionate to it. Kant says that if we were to ask a human being who honors the moral law which kind of world he would create if it were within his power, he would choose a world in which happiness is proportioned to virtue—even if this would mean forfeiting some of his personal happiness as a result should he fail to live up fully to the demands of the moral law (6:5–6). A world in which happiness is proportioned to morality—which Kant calls the "highest good" in the world—therefore represents the final end of human beings, even if morality, strictly speaking, must be determined without reference to any such ends. The idea of the highest good responds to the natural need of the human being to act with reference to an end, but it is also an end that every human as a moral being can endorse.

The problem, of course, is that as far as anyone can tell, happiness is not proportioned to virtue in this world, and it is not within the power of the human being to bring about a state of affairs in which observance of the moral law is the cause of happiness in the world (6:7–8n). In order for this final end (the highest good) to be realized, we must assume the existence of a "higher, moral, most holy, and omnipotent being" who is able to join happiness with worthiness of it (6:5). In this way, "morality inevitably leads to religion" (6:8n). It should be noted that the fact that morality inevitably produces the idea of God does not mean that God's existence can be *proven* on the basis of morality. God is, for Kant, an object of faith, not of knowledge. But this is a *rational* faith insofar as the object of this faith is generated by *practical reason* in the service of the moral end of humanity.

The project of the Religion (6:12–13)

We noted in Chapter 1 that Kant's ethicotheology, as articulated in the first three *Critiques* and very concisely summarized here in the Preface to the first edition, is generated by reason alone without input from historical religion. But the *Religion* is no mere reiteration of this ethicotheology: it accomplishes something quite different, as Kant explains in the Preface to the second edition.

In this Preface, Kant suggests that one can picture the pure religion of reason and historical revelation as two concentric circles, the pure religion of reason constituting the smaller circle within the larger circle of historical revelation. This image suggests not only that there is much in historical revelation that goes beyond the scope of pure rational religion, but also that there is some *overlap* between them, and indeed that the entirety of pure rational religion can be found somewhere within the realm of historical revelation. Here in the Preface, Kant is not yet asserting that this is indeed the relationship between rational and historical religion; such an assertion will have to be substantiated by examining historical revelation in light of moral concepts to see whether they, in fact, overlap and whether there is, therefore, compatibility and unity between reason and revelation. This is precisely what Kant will do in the *Religion*: attempt to determine whether and to what degree pure moral religion can be found in historical revelation.

In a text published several years after the *Religion*, the *Metaphysics of Morals* (1797), Kant gives another explanation of what it means to speak of religion "within the boundaries of mere reason." In this text, he draws a distinction between what he calls the "formal aspect of religion" and "the material aspect of religion." Kant explains that in its formal aspect, religion is "the sum of all duties *as* (*instar*) divine commands," placing emphasis on the *as*. In other words, our moral duties are not moral duties because God commands them; our moral duties are what they are, independently of God. But reason leads to the idea of a God whose commands are at the same time the duties to which we bind ourselves as rational and autonomous beings. Conceived in this way, religion is not a duty *to* God as an externally existing being. And since it is reason and not God which gives us our duties, God's existence is not even required for formal religion, only the *idea* of God generated by practical reason is. (We will say more about this in our discussion of Part III of the *Religion*.) Religion in its formal aspect, then, belongs to "philosophic morals." Religion in its material aspect, by contrast, is "the sum of duties *to (erga)* God," which is to say that it is a service performed for God. As such, it may include commands that go beyond the scope of our moral duties, commands that can only be known by way of empirical, historical revelation. Knowledge that can only come through historical revelation requires the assumption of the actual existence of God, not merely the idea of him generated by practical reason. Religion in its material aspect, therefore, stands outside of philosophic morals (6:487).

After explaining the distinction between the formal and material aspects of religion in the *Metaphysics of Morals*, Kant writes:

> We can indeed speak of a "Religion *within the Boundaries* of Mere Reason," which is not, however, derived *from* reason alone but is also based on the teachings of history and revelation, and considers only the *harmony* of pure practical reason with these (shows that there is no conflict between them). But in that case as well religion is not *pure*; it is rather *religion applied* to a history handed down to us, and there is no place for it in an *ethics* that is pure practical philosophy. (6:488)

In analyzing religion "within the boundaries of mere reason," then, the philosopher indeed goes beyond his small, inner circle of purely philosophical morals into the domain of historical religion. But he does so only to demonstrate the harmony between reason and revelation by "applying" pure religion to history.

As we will see, Kant does indeed believe that there is a harmony between rational and revealed religion, or more specifically, between rational religion and *Christian* revelation. But the *Religion* goes well beyond the simple goal of demonstrating a preexisting harmony between rational and revealed religion; rather it attempts to *create* such harmony. For even if the pure religion of reason sits within the larger circle of historical revelation and therefore overlaps it, there remains much in historical religion that is extraneous to moral religion and, in fact, even *threatens* moral religion. The philosopher, therefore, cannot simply remain indifferent to these nonmoral or amoral elements of historical religion. And so, another key task of the *Religion* is to combat the dangerous elements of revelation through the *moral interpretation of revelation*. Only through such interpretation is it possible to neutralize the threat and put historical faith in the service of moral religion. Accordingly, in *The Conflict of the Faculties*—a text largely written around the time of the *Religion* yet unpublished until after the death of Frederick William II—Kant articulates four rules for the philosophical interpretation of scripture, rules that are utilized extensively in the *Religion*.

> Rule #1: When scripture contains teachings that transcend reason, the philosopher *may* interpret these teachings so that they work in the interest of practical reason; if these teachings contradict practical reason, the philosopher *must* interpret them in the interest of practical reason. (7:38)
>
> Rule #2: Faith in scriptural teachings concerning matters that can only be known through revelation should not be considered meritorious, nor should one be considered guilty for lack of such faith. All that matters in true religion is moral action, and every biblical dogma must be interpreted to reinforce this idea. (7:41–42)
>
> Rule #3: The human being's meritorious actions must be represented as resulting from the use of his own freedom, not from a divine influence to which he is merely passively related. Any scriptural text that suggests the latter view must be interpreted so as to make it consistent with the former. (7:42–43)
>
> Rule #4: The human being is rationally entitled to believe that God will make up for whatever the human being cannot do to make himself righteous—for example, the undoing of his past evil deeds—though reason is *not* entitled to determine what form this divine supplement takes. (7:43–44)

As we will soon see, these four rules of interpretation serve as an effective summary of the main ideas of the *Religion* as a whole, including the imperative to interpret religious doctrines in ways that promote morality; the idea that moral action alone is pleasing to God and constitutes true divine service; the insistence that a human being must make himself what he is to become in a moral sense through the use of his own freedom and not wait passively for divine assistance; and the rational faith that whatever a human being cannot do through his own use of freedom to become righteous will be supplied by God, but only on the condition that the human being has done everything within his power to become a morally good human being.

It is important to keep these rules from the *Conflict* in mind when reading Kant's Preface, because on the basis of the Preface alone, the reader might assume that the task of the *Religion* consists simply in identifying the points of contact between rational and historical religion. But this is only a part of the story. It is, of course, true that, for Kant, Jesus' teachings (understood literally) are one and the same as the teachings of rational religion, so they do not need to be subject to moral-philosophical interpretation to harmonize them with rational religion. But there are plenty of other aspects of Christian scripture and dogma that need to be forcefully interpreted and repurposed in order to bring them in line with rational religion. In fact, some of these teachings are so central to traditional Christian theology that Kant's philosophical engagement with them in the *Religion* was not merely *perceived* as an attack upon Christianity, but undeniably *is* such an attack. As we will see, Kant's radical reinterpretations of central Christian doctrines like original sin or atonement preserve some of the Christian theological idiom, while fully subverting their traditional meanings. No doubt, a central question for any reader of the *Religion* will be how much of Kant's success in demonstrating the harmony between rational and revealed religion is won through the *reduction* of revealed religion to rational religion, a reduction made possible by rules of interpretation not in any way beholden to the literal meaning of revelation.

Part I: Concerning the indwelling of the evil principle alongside the good, or, of the radical evil in human nature

In Part I of the *Religion*, Kant advances his notorious thesis of the "radical evil" in human nature. This idea was certainly controversial in Kant's time because it seemed to be the same old pessimistic Christian doctrine of original sin to which many Enlightenment thinkers were opposed, only dressed up in philosophical garb.

While original sin is a rather complex idea that has undergone many transformations over its long history, it will be sufficient for our purposes to characterize it as follows: The Doctrine of original sin states that the sin that Adam and Eve committed in the Garden of Eden—breaking God's command to refrain from eating the fruit of the Tree of Knowledge of Good and Evil—had a profound effect upon Adam's descendants: as a result of this sin, human nature was fundamentally corrupted, such that all human beings are born with a strong tendency to sin. In fact, living a life without sin is impossible for fallen humanity. Moreover, not only is this sinful nature hereditary; guilt for the sin of Adam and Eve is hereditary as well. This means that all human beings are blameworthy for the sinful nature with which they are born and are, therefore, deserving of divine punishment. As we will see, the one central problem of this doctrine, from Kant's perspective, is that it holds humans morally accountable for a nature with which they are born—and therefore did not freely choose—and for a sin they did not personally commit. Of course, this moral objection to original sin is nothing new; it goes back to Pelagius (late fourth/early fifth century CE), a vocal opponent of one of the principal architects of the doctrine of original sin, St Augustine (d. 430).

Pelagius was deemed a heretic for his belief that humans are not corrupted by nature but have the power to follow God's commands if they so choose; original sin eventually became an orthodox teaching in the Christian Church. Yet, despite its orthodoxy, this doctrine was very much out of step with the general Enlightenment optimism and faith in the rationality and goodness of humanity. And insofar as Kant's doctrine of "radical evil" was seen as nothing more than a philosophical version of this doctrine, Kant himself was subject to criticism. As Goethe said in a letter to Herder: "Kant required a long lifetime to purify his philosophical mantle of many impurities and prejudices. And now he has wantonly tainted it with the shameful stain of radical evil, in order that Christians too might be attracted to kiss its hem" (quoted in Fackenheim, 21). But in fact, Kant's doctrine of radical evil is not a pessimistic one at all; much of Kant's argument in the *Religion* is devoted to the idea that, however evil a human may be, there is always the possibility of moral conversion, and that he can turn toward the good by *his own power*. He is not dependent upon God to *make him good*, and, in fact, if humans must rely upon God to induce this moral conversion, then the conversion has no moral worth anyway; morally good or evil actions, Kant always insists, must be the result of human freedom, or else they are not morally good or evil at all. Far from simply dressing up the doctrine of original sin, Kant is, in fact, offering a very different conception of human evil than the orthodox Christian one.

Nevertheless, as I have already argued, Kant's project in the *Religion* is not simply to throw out revelation and Christian doctrine when it is incompatible with morality. Kant claims that historical religion is a vehicle for the advancement of a pure moral religion. Therefore, the philosopher must make use of historical religion, with its scriptures and dogmas, in order to advance the cause of rational religion. This, however, requires a *philosophical hermeneutics of religion*, in other words, a philosophical interpretation of scripture and doctrine to make it compatible with morality. Kant's thesis of the radical evil of human nature is, then, a reinterpretation of the doctrine of original sin, a reinterpretation that brings it in line with Kant's moral philosophy. For this reason, as we will see, Kant retains certain words that are important in the Christian articulation of the doctrine of original sin—"innate," "natural," and "propensity"— even though in their ordinary meanings they do not fit so well with his notion of moral responsibility. He retains them so as to maintain the connection with the doctrine of original sin, but also defines them in new ways to make them compatible with his moral philosophy. (Kant's unusual use of these terms accounts in part for why Part I of the *Religion* is so challenging to read.)

This is not to say, however, that Part I of the *Religion* is significant only as a philosophical reinterpretation of the doctrine of original sin. Rather, Kant adds here some very important pieces to the ethical theory developed in his previous writings; for this reason, Part I has proven to be of major interest even to those philosophers and students of philosophy who are not especially interested in the philosophy of religion. Much, therefore, has been written about radical evil. Yet in spite of all of this scholarly analysis, Kant's teaching has proven to be notoriously difficult to interpret. In the analysis that follows, I will offer what I take to be the most plausible reading of the text and point the reader to alternate views in the "Guide for Further Reading."

Unfortunately, Kant's analysis in Part I of the radical evil in human nature does not always proceed in the most orderly manner.

Thus, rather than slavishly moving through Part I paragraph by paragraph, I will take the liberty of reorganizing the material somewhat, so that we can answer, on the basis of Kant's text, the three questions that are most central for understanding his argument:

1. What does it mean to say that a human being is evil, and indeed, *radically* evil?
2. How can we know whether a *particular* human being is evil?
3. Is evil characteristic of mankind *as a species*, and how can we know this?

In the course of answering these three questions, I will provide commentary on all of the sections and stages of Kant's argument found in Part I.

1 What does it mean to say that a human being is evil, and indeed, radically evil?

Kant begins Part I with a simple question: Is the world improving, or getting worse? It is a "complaint as old as history" that the world started good (with a Golden Age, or life in Paradise), but has since been declining into evil, such that we now live in the final age and await imminent destruction (6:19). However, more recently, Kant says, a view has emerged among philosophers that the world is, in fact, progressing from bad to better and that the human being is predisposed to such improvement. Kant immediately takes issue with this latter view. If *moral* good or evil is what is in question, he says, then such an optimistic view cannot be based upon experience, for history testifies against this view. Therefore, we must presume that such optimism on the part of these philosophers is simply meant to encourage the development of the "seed of goodness" within us (6:20). Indeed, while Kant insists upon the widespread evil in human society as a rejoinder to the optimistic view, one can safely say that Kant believes that humans are *capable* of improvement; that this improvement is one of the primary concerns of the *Religion* can be clearly seen from the title of Part III: "The Victory of the good principle over the evil principle, and the founding of a kingdom of God on earth."

Is it possible that neither the pessimistic nor the optimistic thesis is true, but rather that as a species, humans are neither good nor evil, or are partly good and partly evil? Kant will reject both of these alternatives; as we will see, his "moral rigorism" dictates that a human being must be good or evil—there is no intermediary or morally neutral state. Kant will argue that humans begin from a state of evil and that this evil is characteristic of the species as a whole. What it means to say that evil is characteristic of the species as a whole and how precisely Kant intends to prove such a strong thesis remain to be seen. First, we must understand what it means, for Kant, to call a human being evil at all.

One common understanding of evil in various philosophical and religious systems is that it originates in inclinations and desires that are a part of our "animal" natures. For however much the rational capacities of mankind seem to raise us above the level of the brute animal, we nevertheless experience inclinations and desires that call into question this supposed superiority: we desire food, sex, and any number of creature comforts; this desire can, at times, overpower our rational faculties and lead us to do "immoral" things. It is, thus, easy to locate the source of evil in these natural desires and inclinations themselves. Kant, however, vigorously resists this view.

For Kant, these natural inclinations cannot be evil in themselves, precisely because they are *natural*. We do not choose to experience such inclinations; they are the result of our natural constitution, of our bodily nature, and therefore not something that we can ever do away with. That being said, the difference between human beings and other animals, for Kant, is that we are not slaves to these inclinations. When an animal experiences an inclination, it acts on it impulsively and instinctively. Humans, however, have the free power of choice (*Willkür*) to act on such a natural inclination or to refrain from doing so. While an animal cannot help but act when an incentive to action presents itself (the stray dog cannot help but snatch the pie off the windowsill), the human being can refrain from acting when an incentive to action presents itself. A hungry human being—or even a sated human being whom nature has endowed with a sweet tooth—will not *inevitably* steal the pie off the windowsill. Rather, he has the power to refrain from doing so and to choose between competing incentives. For example, the desire to not be arrested for theft is a pretty strong counterincentive to stealing a pie, and so, a human might refrain for fear of punishment. But even where punishment is unlikely, a human being might refrain from taking the pie simply because taking the pie would be the *wrong thing to do*, or in more formal language, would represent a *violation of the moral law*.

The moral law, according to Kant, provides its own incentive to action. Humans sometimes refrain from satisfying their natural inclinations and desires because doing so would constitute a lack of respect for the moral law. Nevertheless, respect for the moral law is ultimately just one particular incentive for action among others, even if, as we shall see, it is the one that must be prioritized.

In any case, it is important to bear in mind that for Kant, whatever incentive a human being might be acting upon at any given moment, humans *always act for a reason*; some incentive or other always provides the spring of action. To say that humans always act for a reason is another way of saying that humans always act on *principles*, or what Kant calls *maxims*. Kant defines a maxim as a "rule that the power of choice itself produces for the exercise of its freedom" (6:21). Examples of such rules or practical principles include:

1 Always give ten percent of my paycheck to charity.
2 Always make as much profit as I can in my business transactions without acting unethically.
3 Always make as much profit as I can in my business transactions, even if it means acting unethically, so long as I am not in danger of getting caught.
4 Never wear white after Labor Day.

These are just a sample of maxims that might guide one's actions, and they range from the maxims that are clearly morally good (1 and 2), to a maxim that is clearly morally evil (3), and to a maxim that seems to have nothing to do with morality at all (4). This is precisely the point: maxims are principles that guide any action at all, not just actions with an overt moral content. It is important to keep in mind, however, that a particular practical principle only becomes a maxim once I have *actually adopted that principle* to guide my own actions; the sartorially adventurous, for example, might continue to wear white through the winter, thus rejecting (4). If I do not allow a particular principle to guide my actions, then I have not adopted it as my maxim. Kant's belief that all of our actions are based upon maxims might seem rather odd, since we do not say to ourselves before acting: "I am going to perform such and such an action, as dictated by such and such a maxim." We are not always fully aware at the moment of action what maxim we are acting upon. But Kant would insist, rightly or wrongly, that in those cases in which we are not conscious of our maxims, a bit of self-reflection would reveal that, in fact, there is always an underlying maxim to each of our actions.

To return, then, to the natural inclinations, Kant insists that they are *good*, not exactly in a moral sense—since morality for Kant involves things that we *freely choose*, and we do not freely choose our natural inclinations—but in the sense that they are part of our nature; without them, our higher-order, rational selves would not even exist. Even saints, supposed exemplars of moral perfection, and philosophers, supposed paragons of rational reflection, must eat in order to be moral and rational, so that the natural inclination for food cannot be a bad thing. And without the desire for propagation, our species would not survive for very long. Since these things are part of our nature and the condition of possibility for genuine moral good—that which is the product of our free power of choice—they are a part, Kant says, of our "predisposition to the good." More precisely, they represent the first of three predispositions to the good: animality, humanity, and personality. Kant explains these predispositions in Section I. Let us consider them in turn.

Animality

The predisposition to animality is prerational and belongs to human beings insofar as they have bodies. Kant calls this predisposition "physical or merely *mechanical* self-love, i.e. a love for which reason is not required" (6:26). This mechanical self-love consists in three things: the drive for self-preservation; the desire for the propagation of the species through the sexual drive, and the desire for the preservation of offspring; and the social drive, or the desire for living in a community with other human beings. It is important to note that Kant assigns no moral value to these drives, precisely because they are *natural*, which is to say, not freely chosen by human beings. The presence of these drives does not make a human being evil. And if human beings *only* had this predisposition to animality, then humans could never be considered *moral agents*, anymore than one's cat could be considered a moral agent. So, it is not the case that these drives are in themselves evil; but as we will see, when the satisfaction of these drives is prioritized over the moral law, then moral evil is the result.

Humanity

The predisposition to humanity, like the predisposition to animality, also involves a physical self-love; what distinguishes it, however, is that it involves *comparison*, for which, Kant says, reason is required. The self-love unique to the predisposition to humanity involves a desire for happiness. Yet, happiness is determined only in comparison with others. This kind of self-love gives rise to the inclination to gain worth in the eyes of others, which at first glance seems like a perfectly good thing. Yet, Kant says, this can also lead to a desire to acquire superiority over others and an anxiety that others might be trying to acquire superiority over oneself. Jealously, rivalry, and secret or open hostility toward others may result. Nevertheless, nature wants us to use such competitiveness as an incentive for the development of *culture*. Therefore, while the predisposition to humanity can result in evil when misused (much like the predisposition to animality), it is this misuse that is evil, not the predisposition itself.

Personality

Kant does not use the word "personality" in the way we ordinarily use it, to refer to the individual temperament or character of a particular person. We commonly speak of different people as having different personalities, but Kant uses the word to refer to something that is possessed equally by every human being, and that can even be said to constitute the essence of what it means to be a human being. Kant describes the predisposition to personality as "the susceptibility to respect for the moral law *as of itself a sufficient incentive to the power of choice*." In other words, the predisposition to personality belongs to the human being *as a moral being*. For Kant, in order for a human being to choose the moral law over self-love, or in other words, to choose the good over evil, there must be a predisposition in him to choose the moral law for its own sake. Kant calls this a "moral feeling," which is the feeling of respect for the moral law. Having this moral feeling, of course, does not in itself make the human being good. Freely making this moral feeling the sole incentive in the use of one's power of choice, as we will see, is what makes a human being good.

It is important to note that even though the predispositions to animality and humanity lead to vice when they are not made subservient to the moral law, this does not mean that these predispositions should be eradicated. Indeed, Kant insists that they *cannot* be eradicated, because they are a necessary feature of human nature. Moreover, it is not simply the case that we have to just grin and bear the predispositions to animality and humanity because we cannot eradicate them; Kant insists that they are *good* in themselves, and it is only the bad use we make of them that results in evil. These predispositions are a necessary rather than contingent feature of human nature, meaning that human beings would cease to be human beings without them. The predisposition to animality is necessary to ensure the survival of man as a living being; and without the rationality that constitutes the predisposition to humanity, mankind could only ever act immediately upon instinct, without the ability to form, plan, and attain long-range goals, including happiness.

Evil is not the result, then, of the natural inclinations themselves, but rather the result of improper prioritization of our incentives. For Kant, the incentive of the moral law—an incentive that all humans experience, since receptiveness to the moral law is part of what it means to be a human being—must take priority over any other incentives. The moral law demands unconditional respect; it is to take priority over every other incentive. It is only when I have given the moral law priority that I can then act upon other incentives to satisfy my natural inclinations in good conscience. It is not wrong for me to satisfy my natural inclination by eating pie, but I can only do so, provided that I do not violate the moral law in satisfying my inclination. If I steal the pie off the windowsill, I have prioritized the satisfaction of my inclinations over the moral law. In Kant's terms, I have prioritized the *incentive of self-love* over the *incentive of the moral law*. In sum, Kant does not expect humans to deny or constrain or eliminate their inclinations altogether but only to refrain from satisfying such inclinations when doing so would violate the moral law.

With this in mind, let us return briefly to the issue of maxims. In the opening paragraphs of Part I, Kant writes that we can consider a human being to be evil not because he performs evil actions (actions that violate the moral law) but because his actions are "so constituted that they allow the inference of evil maxims in him" (6:20). This point is, in fact, quite intuitive; we know from ordinary experience that a specific action that a human being performs is not necessarily a reliable guide to whether that person has acted in an evil way. For example, if I jump a subway turnstile and enter the subway car without buying a ticket, I have acted contrary to the law. And indeed, if my action is guided by a maxim to "Take free rides on public transit whenever I can do so without being caught," then my action is evil. But if I perform this very same action because I see an elderly woman being mugged in the subway car and I want to come to her aid as quickly as possible, then this action clearly ceases to be an evil one. An action can really only be good or evil on the basis of the particular maxim that governs it.

Let's say that I do make it my maxim to take free rides on public transit whenever I can do so without getting caught; does this make me an evil person? This is a difficult question. Even if everyone agrees that taking free rides on public transit is morally reprehensible, many might be reluctant to call a person who does so evil simply on the basis of this maxim. For, this maxim is certainly not as reprehensible as other maxims that a person might hold ("Always mug old ladies when no one is watching," for example). In any case, this one bad maxim, or even several bad maxims, might be counterbalanced or outweighed by any number of other morally commendable maxims that this person might hold. Perhaps it would be best to say that such a person is a mix of good and evil, good in some ways and bad in others, or perhaps even morally neutral if the good and evil balance each other out. This, however, is not a position that Kant accepts. Let's see why.

We have already seen that for Kant, the moral law is unconditional; it demands that all other incentives be subordinated to the incentive of the moral law itself. In other words, the demands of the moral law are so stringent as to allow *no exceptions*. Even allowing oneself a single exception to this unconditional demand means placing the incentive of self-love above the incentive of the moral law.

If this is indeed the case, as Kant believes, then there are really only two options for the human being: unconditionally prioritizing the moral law (in which case one is good) or allowing oneself to make exceptions, or even a single exception to the moral law when one sees fit (in which case one is evil). Whether I have one bad maxim or all of my maxims are bad, in either case, I have compromised the unconditional demand of the moral law, and to that extent I am evil.

It is important not to misunderstand Kant here. This does not mean that all evil people are equally evil or that we cannot distinguish the turnstile jumper from Hitler; that would be absurd. Kant does believe, however, that the demand of the moral law is unconditional and that as beings with free will, it is indeed possible for us to live up to this unconditional demand. Therefore, failure to do so constitutes a truly *moral* failure on our part, which Kant does not hesitate to call evil. While the turnstile jumper and Hitler may differ greatly in the degree to which they prioritize self-love over the moral law, they both do so and are evil on account of it.

One interesting feature of Kant's moral rigorism is that, ultimately, one is good or evil on the basis of a single choice, which Kant calls a supreme maxim: the choice either to unconditionally prioritize the moral law or the choice to allow an exception to the moral law whenever one sees fit. A person who chooses the moral law over self-love has a good supreme maxim and is, therefore, a good person, one who will, on account of this supreme maxim, form particular maxims of action that are themselves good; a person who chooses self-love over the moral law has an evil supreme maxim and is, therefore, an evil person, and will, on account of this supreme maxim, occasionally form particular maxims of action that are themselves bad.

Kant's initial definition of evil, then—that humans can be called evil because their actions allow the inference of evil maxims—is not the whole story. A particular evil maxim that governs a particular evil action is really just a symptom of an underlying evil supreme maxim. In fact, it is this evil supreme maxim that makes a human being evil. This is why Kant adds, just a few lines after this initial definition, that in order to call a human being evil, it must be possible to make an inference from even one consciously evil action to an evil maxim that underlies it, and then from this evil maxim to "the presence in the subject of a common ground, itself a maxim, of all particular morally evil maxims" (6:20). This common ground of all particular morally evil maxims is the supreme maxim that consists in allowing oneself to prioritize the incentive of self-love over the incentive of the moral law when one sees fit to do so.

In the "Remark" appended to this opening section of Part I (beginning at 6:22), Kant introduces an extremely important term, *disposition* (*Gesinnung*). He defines it as the "first subjective ground of the adoption of maxims" and refers to the good or evil disposition as "the inner principle of maxims." What does this mean? In essence, the disposition is nothing other than that supreme maxim discussed above, which consists in the maxim to subordinate either self-love to the moral law or the moral law to self-love. One can be said to have a good disposition if one prioritizes the moral law and an evil disposition if one prioritizes self-love. The disposition is called the first subjective ground of the adoption of maxims, or the inner principle of maxims, precisely because it is this fundamental decision regarding the priority of the moral law or of self-love that guides one's subsequent maxim formation.

In an important article, "The Ethical Significance of Kant's *Religion*," John Silber argues that Kant's concept of the disposition is perhaps the most important contribution of the *Religion* to Kant's ethical theory, because it accounts for the continuity of the moral subject. This is an important insight. As we have seen, Kant resists the hypothesis that the human being is somehow partly good and partly evil. Yet, at first blush, this seems to be a very strong hypothesis, precisely because it accurately reflects our experience of what people are really like. Even the best people are never completely free of any moral wrongdoing and even the worst do not do evil all the time. So, it would initially seem plausible to say that there is a mixture of good and evil in people.

But this hypothesis presents some difficulties. Should I say that I am good when doing good things and evil when doing evil things? This would mean that my moral character potentially changes from action to action. We do not tend to think that bad people are only bad when they are doing bad things; it seems that somehow or other, their "badness" is precisely what makes it possible for them to do evil at any moment. So, there must be a way to account for an enduring moral character behind the individual actions. The maxims present themselves as candidates to account for this enduring moral character. Can we say that a person is bad when he holds a bad maxim and good when he holds a good maxim? The problem is that any one human being holds many different maxims and not all of them are bad. I may decide that I will violate the moral law for the sake of money but not of sexual gratification, because sexual gratification is not sufficiently important to me to warrant violation of the moral law. If we used maxims as the guide to determining whether a human being is good or evil, we might well be led to conclude that humans are a mix of good and evil.

Yet, the disposition, according to Kant, can only be good or evil, not both, precisely because it involves a single choice between two alternatives, subordinating self-love to the moral law or the moral law to self-love. Because the disposition involves a single choice, this alone provides a basis for calling the human being good or evil. Moreover, an evil disposition is perfectly compatible with a human being holding some good maxims and some evil ones and performing some good actions and some evil actions. For, we have seen that an evil person does not have to have *all* bad maxims, though he has at least one. Holding some bad maxims and being an evil person is perfectly consistent, in Kant's view, with holding some other good maxims. As Silber notes, it is the continuity of the disposition that makes possible a moral self-identity: "Our moral self-consciousness would be fractured and dissipated into isolated intentions and actions if we did not relate them to one another by reference to their common ground of intention in disposition" (cxvii–cxviii). The notion of the disposition, then, provides the basis for speaking of an enduring good or evil character in the human being. And this good or evil disposition consists in nothing other than the choice of a good or evil supreme maxim.

Of course, Kant does not speak simply of the *evil* of human nature but of the *radical* evil. What precisely does Kant mean by radical evil? This phrase certainly conjures up images of *extreme* evil, the kind we associate with Hitler or Osama bin Laden. But this, in fact, is not at all what Kant means. All that Kant means here is that this evil is based upon a fundamental choice, on the level of the disposition, to subordinate the moral law to self-love; evil is not radical in the sense of *extreme*, but radical in the sense of going to the *root* of human action, the fundamental choice of maxim that subsequently influences our choice of particular maxims.

Before moving on to our next question, namely, how one can know whether a human being is, in fact, evil, we should briefly consider what Kant calls "diabolical evil," a topic that comes up in Section III. Here, Kant famously denies that humans are capable of acting diabolically. What exactly does this mean? In essence, diabolical evil is evil that is done for its own sake; one violates the moral law simply for the sake of violating the moral law. To put it differently, violation of the moral law is its own incentive for one who acts diabolically. Kant thinks that such diabolical action is not possible for a human being. Why not?

Kant reiterates (6:34–35) that evil is not rooted in the sensuous nature of human beings or in the natural inclinations and desires that result from this sensuous nature, precisely because humans are not responsible for this sensuous nature. Something can properly be called evil only when it results from the free power of choice of the human being; this point should be clear by now. Furthermore, Kant says that evil is not the result of "corruption" of our moral reason, because such a corruption of moral reason—whereby the dignity of the law would be wiped out—is impossible (6:35). There are two reasons why reason cannot extirpate the dignity of the moral law: one that is simple and one that is more complex. The simple reason is that it is constitutive of human nature, according to Kant, that the moral law is experienced as an incentive of action. This is nothing other than the predisposition to *personality* discussed above, a predisposition to the good that is a necessary feature of the human being. Therefore, if a human were to cease experiencing the moral law as worthy of respect (even when violating the moral law), then the human would cease to be human.

The more complex explanation for why reason cannot extirpate the dignity of the moral law is that if one fails to experience the moral law as an incentive to action, then one *ceases to be free* and therefore *ceases to be morally responsible*. Let's examine this more closely. The natural world, according to Kant, operates according to fixed *laws*, the laws of nature. These laws are *deterministic*, which is to say that they invariably dictate what will happen in the universe from one moment to the next. But free human action is an exception to this natural determinism. As a free being, how I act at any moment is not simply determined by the laws of nature but is determined *by me*, independently of those laws. In this sense, freedom represents a different kind of causality than the causality present in nature. But the fact that freedom does not operate according to the *laws of nature* does not mean that freedom is altogether *lawless*. If there were no laws governing the use of freedom, no causes at all that determine free actions, then these free actions would be entirely *random*. Rather, there is a law that governs the use of freedom, and for Kant, this law is the moral law itself (or practical reason). To act freely is to act according to the moral law. There is an important consequence to this line of thinking: if acting freely means acting according to the moral law, then a corruption of the morally legislative reason would amount to the destruction of freedom itself. If a human being were to lose this morally legislative reason (let's say through brain injury or mental disability), then this person would, according to Kant's argument, cease to be free and therefore cease to be *responsible* for his own actions. So, evil (and this is the main point) *cannot* result from a corruption of the morally legislative reason, because such a corruption would mean that the person is no longer a free and responsible being, in which case *evil can no longer be imputed to him*.

Such morally legislative reason, then, will always remain intact in the human being, otherwise he would cease to be human. As such, the moral law will always function as an incentive to action, even when he chooses to prioritize another incentive over it. This is the important point: because the moral law will always be an incentive, a human being will only ever violate the moral law because of a competing incentive, never just "for the hell of it," as Peter Fenves quips (79). Violation of the moral law can never serve as its own incentive; this is what Kant means when he says that humans are not capable of acting diabolically.

2 How can we know whether a particular *human being is evil?*

As we move to the second and third questions, the relevant pieces of Kant's text become substantially less clear, and contested interpretations abound in the scholarly literature. To see this, let us return to a passage to which we have already referred but have not yet fully probed. At 6:20, Kant says that we cannot observe maxims, even our own, and therefore, we cannot reliably make a judgment about whether a particular human being is evil on the basis of experience. Yet, Kant says, it must be possible for us to make an inference from one or more consciously evil actions to an underlying evil maxim, and from this maxim, to the presence of a common ground of all evil maxims; and this underlying common ground of all maxims, Kant adds, is itself a maxim. To make sense of these claims, let's begin with Kant's remark that we cannot *observe* maxims. This seems clear enough; we can obviously *see* actions that people perform, but we cannot see the maxims that govern those particular actions. At most, we can make an inference about the maxim from the action or from other things we *can* observe. For example, I may not be able to see the maxim of the turnstile jumper directly, but I certainly know that the maxim governing his action was a good one if I watch him rush to the aid of the elderly woman. But what if there is no elderly woman? What if he just gets on the subway car and sits down? Now I certainly have reason to suspect that his maxim is a bad one. But can I be sure? Maybe he needed to catch the train because some emergency situation was waiting for him at the next subway stop, in which case getting there as quickly as possible would certainly take priority over paying the subway fare. So let's say I follow him to his next stop to see whether he is rushing to intervene in some life-or-death matter. If he gets off the subway and rushes off to the movie theater so as not to miss the beginning of the film, then I can pretty confidently infer that his maxim was a bad one. Yet, while it seems theoretically possible to make an inference from actions to underlying maxims, as in this case, it must be admitted that I might not have all of the information to do so (or not have the time to follow the turnstile jumper to his destination!). It may well be the case that I can never be completely certain, and the best I can conclude is that a person *probably* has an evil maxim.

There are some cases, however, in which it may well be impossible to know whether someone has a good maxim or not, particularly in cases in which doing the right thing also involves the satisfaction of nonmoral inclinations. Let's say I happen to find a lost wallet. I know that returning the wallet is the right thing to do, but the wallet has cash in it, which I know I can keep easily enough without getting caught. Here, the incentive of the moral law comes into conflict with a nonmoral incentive. Now, let's alter the scenario a bit: I find the wallet and recall having seen a sign offering a reward to whoever finds and returns the very same wallet. In this situation, I can get some cash and also do what the law requires; it is a win-win situation. But an observer might wonder: have I returned the wallet strictly because it was the right thing to do, or have I only done so because there was a reward involved, in which case I have really acted out of self-love? It seems that there is no way for an outside observer to tell for sure. In fact, it may not even be possible for *me* to know whether I am acting out of a good maxim like "Always return lost property to its owner" or out of an evil one like "Only return lost property when there is a reward involved." And yet, whether my action is good or evil really depends upon which maxim I am acting upon in this situation. If I do what the law requires but not because it is the right thing to do, then in Kant's language I am acting merely "in conformity with the law" or "in conformity with duty" (*pflichtmässig*) but not "out of respect for the law" or "out of duty" (*aus Pflicht*). It is only the latter which counts as genuinely moral action; the former is merely the *appearance* of morality.

It is probably these cases—in which a person acts in conformity with the law but it is not clear whether he acts out of respect for the law—that Kant has in mind when he says that we cannot "unproblematically" observe maxims "even in ourselves." This does not mean that we can *never* know what our own maxims are or whether we are acting morally or not. What is so problematic about such self-knowledge for Kant is that humans have a tendency to deceive themselves regarding their true intentions. In Section III, Kant speaks of "a certain *perfidy* on the part of the human heart," which consists in deceiving ourselves concerning our own dispositions and not taking the trouble to conscientiously examine our dispositions so long as we are *conforming* to the moral law (6:38). As long he has done what the moral law requires, such a person does not trouble himself regarding whether such an action was done strictly out of respect for the law—making the incentive of the law itself the supreme spring of action—or merely in conformity with it, with some other incentive playing the dominant role. Kant adds that through this dishonesty we "throw dust in our own eyes," thereby hindering a genuine moral disposition from taken hold within us (ibid.). It should be noted, however, that Kant goes on to say that this dishonesty and self-deception "rests on the radical evil of human nature" and "constitutes the foul stain of our species" (ibid.)—harsh language that ultimately makes us responsible and morally accountable for this self-deception. Therefore, if we cannot perceive our own maxims "unproblematically," it is not because our own maxims are, in principle, unknowable to ourselves but only because of a lack of diligence in investigating our true motives.

It seems to be difficult, then, though not entirely impossible, to infer a particular evil maxim from an action that is contrary to the moral law. In some cases, our knowledge of the maxims of others is at best probabilistic; in other cases, it can be quite impossible to infer the maxim from a particular action, particularly if the action is in conformity with the law. In principle, however, we should be able to identify our own maxims, even if humans very often deceive themselves regarding their true motives. Assuming we know that a human being has a particular evil maxim, can we then infer from this particular evil maxim an evil disposition, an evil supreme maxim? It certainly seems that this is the case. While we cannot "see" the supreme maxim any more than we can see a particular maxim, the presence of a particular evil maxim would have to mean, by Kant's rigorist logic, that the person under consideration has allowed himself to make at least one exception to the moral law, which he would have not done if he had made the moral law a sufficient and unconditional incentive in his supreme maxim. According to Kant's logic, then, we can infer an evil disposition from a particular evil maxim, though we would have to acknowledge that we can only be as sure of the disposition as we are of the particular maxim from which we are making the inference. Any uncertainty accompanying our move from the action to the particular maxim would have to accompany the inference from the particular maxim to the supreme one, as well.

3 Is evil characteristic of mankind as a species, and how can we know this?

At the end of Section III, Kant comments on the saying that "every man has his price." If this is true, Kant says—that there is no one with an incorruptible degree of virtue—then what the Apostle says may indeed be universally true of human beings: "There is no distinction here, they are all under sin—there is none righteous (in the spirit of the law), no, not one." The apostle Kant quotes here is Paul, from the Letter to the Romans (3.9-10). Paul insists that sin is truly universal—there is no one who is free from it. In Christian theology, the universality of sin is understood to result from the fact that all are born with original sin, the corrupted nature that predisposes humanity to sin. As I said at the beginning of this chapter, Kant's doctrine of radical evil represents, in the context of the larger project of the *Religion*, a philosophical reinterpretation of the doctrine of original sin, one that brings it in line with morality. I also suggested that one of the main problems with the doctrine of original sin from a Kantian perspective is that since we are *born with it*, we really cannot be said to be *responsible for it*. Not only does it therefore not count as genuine *moral* evil (which can only be the product of the free power of choice), but it would be unjust of God to punish us for it. Kant insists throughout Part I that humans are indeed free and therefore have it fully within their power to refrain from evil.

If evil results from freedom, then it stands to reason that it is possible for a human being to live a life free from sin; even if no one has, in fact, done so, it would have to at least remain a possibility that some human beings could be free from sin. It seems, then, that according to Kant's understanding of evil, one cannot reasonably make the claim, as Paul does, that *everyone* is guilty of sin. Even if this claim were true, it would be impossible to verify; we would have to have empirical knowledge that every human being who ever lived had actually acted contrary to the moral law. This is certainly not knowledge we are in a position to have. Moreover, we would have to be able to successfully infer from that action contrary to the moral law an underlying evil maxim, which, as we have already seen, may not always be possible to do. So, it seems that the claim that all humans are evil is an impossible one to verify, given Kant's understanding of evil. And yet, Kant defends this very claim. To see how and why he does this, we need to carefully examine what Kant means when he says that there is radical evil in human *nature*, that this evil is *innate*, and that humans thereby have a *propensity* to evil. We will consider these three words (nature, innate, and propensity) in turn.

Nature

At 6:21, Kant comments on the meaning of the word "nature," which appears in the title of Part I in the phrase, "the radical evil in human nature." Kant anticipates that the reader might take exception to the idea that humans are evil by nature and acknowledges that the word "nature" stands in contradiction to the predicates "morally good" and "morally evil," assuming that by "nature" we mean the opposite of what arises through the use of freedom (6:21). In other words, insofar as nature is the opposite of freedom, we cannot speak of someone being evil by nature, so long as we are using the word "nature" in the ordinary sense. This is a clue, of course, that Kant is not using the word "nature" in the ordinary sense. What does he mean, then, when he speaks of radical evil in human nature? Kant goes on to say that with the phrase "the nature of the human being," he is referring to the "subjective ground . . . of the exercise of the human being's freedom in general (under objective moral laws) antecedent to every deed that falls within the scope of the senses" (ibid.). This hardly clarifies matters; what is this "subjective ground" of the exercise of human freedom? In fact, it is nothing other than the supreme maxim itself. Kant says that this subjective ground must be "a deed of freedom" (something freely chosen by the human being); otherwise it could not be called "evil." Therefore, the ground of evil cannot result from anything that determines our power of choice through the natural inclinations but only from a "rule that the power of choice itself produces for the exercise of its freedom"—in other words, a *maxim* (ibid.). Therefore, to say that a person is evil by nature amounts to saying that he has freely chosen an evil supreme maxim—a choice, as we know, that precedes any particular evil action and, indeed, represents the first use of the power of choice, insofar as every particular maxim and every particular action presuppose a fundamental decision to prioritize or subordinate the incentive of the moral law.

It appears, then, that the word "nature," as Kant uses it, actually means the very opposite of "nature" as it is ordinarily used, precisely because this "nature" is freely chosen! But, in fact, there is one more crucial point that Kant adds concerning his use of the word "nature": Whenever we say, Kant writes, that a human being is good or evil *by nature*, it only means that the human being "holds within himself a first ground (to us inscrutable) for the adoption of good or evil (unlawful) maxims, and that he holds this ground *qua* human, universally—in such a way, therefore, that by his maxims he expresses at the same time the character of his species" (6:21). In fact, then, there is a component of Kant's use of the word "nature" that is like the ordinary usage: whenever we say "the human being is X by nature," we usually mean that this X is a universal feature of the species as such. Kant preserves precisely this component of the word's meaning; even though this good or evil is *freely chosen* and therefore not "natural" in the ordinary sense, it is nevertheless the case that in freely choosing a good or evil supreme maxim, whatever the human being chooses happens also to be the same thing that every other member of the species chooses.

Of course, in defining what he means by the word "nature," Kant has not committed himself at this point in the *Religion* to the claim that evil is, in fact, natural to humans as a species (though the title of Part I gives away his ultimate position on the issue). Kant will soon make some more comments relevant to the issue of whether or not humans are evil as a species. But before looking at those passages, we need to comment on the two other terms that, like "nature," Kant uses in very unusual ways: "innate" and "propensity."

Innate

At 6:21–22, right after his discussion of the word "nature," Kant comments that he will say of this good or evil (whichever it turns out to be) characteristic of the human being that it is *innate* in him. But again, just like the word "nature," the word "innate" is a bad fit here. Usually, when we say that something is "innate," we mean that it was something we are born with or born into (*innatus* is the past participle of the Latin verb *innasci*, "to be born in/into"). In this sense, something that is innate is beyond our control and therefore not imputable to us. So, it would have been perfectly sensible for Kant to avoid the word "innate" with reference to the good or evil disposition. Yet, Kant uses it, I suggest, for the same reason he retains the word "nature," because he is attempting to reformulate the doctrine of original sin so that it fits within practical reason. Recall that original sin, according to Christian doctrine, is innate in the literal sense of the word; it is something that every human being is born with or born into. However, Kant cannot accept that original sin is innate in the literal sense, because he believes that humans cannot be morally accountable for anything that they do not freely do. So, if he wishes to refer to the disposition as "innate," he must redefine this word as well. And this is precisely what he does; to possess a good or evil disposition as an *innate* characteristic does not mean that the human being has not earned this disposition but simply that "it has not been earned in time (that he has been one way or the other *always, from his youth on*)."

How are we to understand this? On the one hand, the claim that the disposition has not been earned in time reflects an idea that is central to Kant's thought, that space and time belong only to the domain of natural causality and that the free will, insofar as it is not a part of the domain of natural causality, is somehow outside of space and time. In this sense, Kant can say that the disposition, because it is a product of freedom, "has not been earned in time." We can perhaps also understand Kant's claim, however, without making recourse to his distinction between the phenomenal realm of nature and the noumenal realm of freedom. Simply stated, the fundamental decision to prioritize the moral law over self-love or self-love over the moral law must have been made at the very first moment that the human being could properly be said to be free. Only a free being experiences the incentive of the moral law, and therefore, there is no freedom without such an experience. The experience of freedom is the experience of the moral law, and the very first use of this freedom, at whatever stage in infant or child development it might be said to occur, already involves this decision regarding the relative priorities of moral law and self-love. In this sense, the disposition is as old as the first manifestation of freedom in the human being. It is for this reason that Kant says that we can call the disposition "innate."

At 6:25–26, after having explained what he means by the words "nature" and "innate," Kant makes an interesting remark. He says that whether we can consider humans to be good or evil not simply as individuals but as a whole species can only be determined later if it so happens that "anthropological research" gives us grounds for making such an attribution. This is a rather puzzling claim. Unfortunately, Kant does not explain precisely what he means by "anthropological research" or exactly how such anthropological research could contribute to answering the question. But insofar as this anthropological research is conducted empirically, it would seem impossible for it to furnish an answer to this question; as we have already discussed, it is impossible to empirically validate the claim that all members of the human species begin their free lives in a state of radical evil. For this reason, this remark about "anthropological research" has left many readers of Kant scratching their heads. Kant does not say anything further on the matter here. But he will say more in his discussion of the "propensity to evil," to which we now turn.

Propensity

Kant's discussion of the "propensity to evil in human nature" in Section II is certainly among the most challenging pieces of Part I of the *Religion*. To make sense of his argument, we first have to understand what he means by "propensity." We then have to analyze the "three grades" of the propensity to evil: frailty, impurity, and depravity. As with the words "nature" and "innate," Kant's unorthodox use of these words can be quite confusing.

Kant defines "propensity" as the "subjective ground of the possibility of an inclination (habitual desire, *concupiscentia*), insofar as this possibility is contingent for humanity in general" (6:29). This definition could hardly be considered helpful, but we can tease out the meaning. First of all, we see that a propensity is what makes a particular inclination possible. My inclination for lollipops, for example, must in some way result from a propensity I have for the enjoyment of sweets. So, propensities are not universal, any more than the desires or inclinations that they make possible are universal. Not everyone shares my propensity for sweets or my inclination for lollipops. This is what Kant indicates when he says, in the final clause of his definition, that "this possibility [of an inclination] is contingent for humanity in general"; "contingent" here means precisely *not universally shared by human beings*, not a necessary component of essence of the human being. This point is further clarified in Kant's rather offensive footnote to this definition, where he writes that propensity is only a predisposition to the enjoyment of something that, once it is actually experienced, arouses an inclination to it. By way of illustration, Kant writes that "all savages" have a propensity for intoxicants, and they, therefore, have no desire for intoxicants until they have tried it, at which point their desire for intoxicants becomes "almost inextinguishable." There are two important points that Kant is making here. First, propensities are not universal since, as Kant insists, savages have at least one propensity (for intoxicants) not shared by (all) "civilized" peoples. Second, a propensity is really the *potential* for an inclination, even if this potential is not yet "activated"; I may have a propensity for sweets, but if I had never had anything sweet in my life, I certainly wouldn't be walking around with a hankering for candy. However, once I have my first piece, what was at first only a propensity becomes an inclination.

It should be clear that propensity as defined here is different from the three predispositions to the good (animality, humanity, and personality) insofar as those predispositions are not contingent, but rather a necessary and universal feature of human nature. But even if propensities are not universal, we normally think of them as something we are born with and therefore not ultimately within our control. Kant indicates as much when he writes that a propensity is distinguished from a predisposition insofar as a propensity "can indeed be innate yet *may* be represented as not being such: it can rather be thought of (if it is good) as *acquired*, or (if evil) as *brought* by the human being *upon* himself" (6:29). It is not clear why Kant thinks that if a propensity is innate (in the ordinary sense of something the human being is born with), it "*may* be represented" as something for which the human being is responsible. Is Kant simply acknowledging here that even though propensities are innate, people are commonly praised or condemned for them anyway? In any case, the point seems to be that a propensity, *ordinarily understood*, is something for which the human being can hardly be held morally responsible. It is for this reason that Kant signals that he is using the word in a different way, claiming that he is only speaking of a propensity to "genuine," *moral* evil, which must ultimately be seated in the "subjective ground of the possibility of the deviation of the maxims from the moral law" (6:29). As he did with the terms "nature" and "innate," Kant insists that the propensity to evil, contrary to common usage, must originate in the free power of choice. He adds that if we can indeed assume (as he does) that this propensity belongs to all human beings and is therefore characteristic of the species, we can then call this propensity a "*natural* propensity" to evil (again, Kant is using the word "natural" in his own unique way here).

In this final paragraph of Section II, Kant notes that there are two kinds of propensity: physical and moral (this corresponds to the word "propensity" according to ordinary usage and according to Kant's own special usage). A physical propensity, Kant says, can influence a human's power of choice insofar as he is a natural being. But it does not make sense to say that there is a physical propensity to *moral evil*: moral evil can only originate from freedom; but a physical propensity, since it is "based on sensory inducements," is not free. Therefore, to talk of a physical propensity to moral evil is, Kant says, a contradiction. If there is such a thing as a propensity to moral evil, this propensity must be something we freely choose, and that constitutes our own deed (6:31).

Kant immediately comments, however, that it is strange to talk of a propensity as though it were our own *deed*, precisely because we ordinarily think of a propensity as something that *precedes* every deed and which therefore is not itself a deed (6:31). So, it seems that we cannot talk about a moral propensity, or a propensity to evil. How does Kant get around this problem?

Kant's solution is to say that we can take the word "deed" itself in two different ways. We can use the word, as we ordinarily do, to refer to the specific actions we take, as determined by our maxims and by our underlying disposition; or, we can use the word to refer to our free choice of the supreme maxim itself. In this latter sense, the propensity to evil is a deed, since it is something we freely choose, but it can also be considered a "propensity" because it constitutes the formal ground of each of our evil actions (deeds in the ordinary sense) (6:31). The propensity to evil, therefore, is once again nothing other than the evil deed consisting in the choice of the supreme maxim to subordinate the moral law to self-love. This evil deed is not a deed in the ordinary sense, however; it is not an action performed in time and empirically visible to others or ourselves (it is not a deed in the manner that stealing a lollipop from a child is a deed). Rather, it is the choice of the supreme maxim, a choice that is not visible to others or ourselves because it is not made in time (since it belongs to the realm of freedom rather than to natural causality). This propensity is a deed (though not in the usual sense) for which we are responsible because it is the product of our free power of choice. However, it can still be called a "propensity" to evil because it makes possible the subsequent adoption of particular evil maxims and actual evil deeds performed in time.

The reader should notice the Latin phrases that Kant puts in parentheses in the passage quoted above. Kant calls this propensity to evil *peccatum originarium*: original sin. By contrast, the actual evil deed that a human performs (in the ordinary sense—like stealing a lollipop from a child) is called a *peccatum derivativum*: derivative sin. Thus, Kant's philosophical reformulation of the doctrine of original sin preserves an important facet of the doctrine, which is that original sin is something that is imputable to us (on account of which we are guilty), and yet it is not a specific empirical deed we perform, but a sinful "nature" that conditions the commission of actual sinful actions. The difference, of course, is that this sinful nature is not something that is *inherited through birth*, but rather is the result of our own free choice.

With this understanding of what Kant means by a "propensity to evil" in human nature, we can now turn to the three grades of the propensity to evil.

Frailty

Kant writes that, when one experiences frailty, one incorporates the moral law into the maxim of one's power of choice; and yet, despite being an irresistible incentive to action "objectively" or "ideally," the moral law is nevertheless weaker than the incentives supplied by the natural inclinations when it comes to actually following that maxim (6:29). This, says Kant, is what Paul is expressing in Romans 7.15 when he exclaims: "What I would, that I do not!" It is worth noting that for many Christian interpreters of Paul's words, this weakness of the will is the direct result of original sin.

What Kant describes as frailty sounds much like "weakness of the will": one knows the good, wants to do the good, but fails to do so. But it is not clear that Kant's ethical theory can account for such a phenomenon. For what, exactly, could cause the will to be weak? Certainly, it cannot be that complying with the law is beyond the capacity of such a person; otherwise his failure to comply would not be imputable, and therefore, it would make no sense to call it a grade of the "propensity to evil." Frailty can only be, then, lack of resolve to actually comply in practice with the maxims that one forms in theory.

Impurity

Like frailty, impurity is also compatible with a good maxim. In fact, even though this is a "worse" grade of evil than that of frailty, impurity itself does not even involve actions that are contrary to the moral law! Impurity of the heart, Kant says, is when one forms a maxim that is good insofar as it intends compliance with the law but is not *purely* moral because the law alone does not constitute a sufficient incentive for compliance; rather, one needs additional, nonmoral incentives (6:30). Impurity, then, does not involve actions that are contrary to the law. Instead, my action is legal, and even my maxim is good in a sense, insofar as it is my intention to comply with the moral law. But the moral law is not my *sole* incentive, and, in fact, the nonmoral incentive is playing such a strong role that without the presence of the nonmoral incentive, I would likely fail to follow the moral law. An example of impurity, then, is one whose maxim would be to return the lost wallet and yet would fail to do so without the supplementary incentive of the reward.

One might well ask how Kant can insist that someone has a good maxim when he clearly fails to give priority to the incentive of the moral law and acts merely in conformity with duty in requiring other, nonmoral incentives. Far from a second stage in the descent into depravity, it seems that "impurity," as Kant describes it, is really inconsistent with holding a good maxim in the first place. But it is important to bear in mind that Kant says that the maxim is only good insofar as it intends *compliance* with the law—in other words, insofar as it intends *legality*. The maxim is not a good one in the truest sense, insofar as it does not intend compliance purely out of respect for the moral law.

One might also wonder why impurity represents a higher degree of the propensity to evil than frailty does; after all, a frail person has failed to even act in conformity with the law, which the impure person at least manages to do. John Silber suggests an answer when he writes that impurity "does not even know that it follows the law without ever obeying it," whereas "the weak-willed individual [frailty] is strengthened by the knowledge of weakness and purified" by the self-condemnation of his vice (cxxii). While the actual violation of the moral law in deed awakens one to his own frailty, the impure person's conformity to the moral law silences, or at least potentially silences, his self-condemnation, thus paving the way for a good conscience in the face of his own evil.

Depravity

While frailty and impurity are compatible with a good maxim—at least insofar as the maxim intends compliance with the law—depravity is the propensity of the human being to form evil maxims, subordinating the moral law to self-love. This depravity, Kant writes, can be called "perversity" of the heart, since it consists in a reversal of the proper order of incentives determining the free power of choice, subordinating the moral law to self-love (6:30). It is important to remember that I can subordinate the moral law to self-love and therefore be an evil person—guilty of perversity of the human heart—without ever performing an action that violates the moral law. One acts in conformity with duty (*pflichtmässig*) but not out of duty (*aus Pflicht*), or in terms that Kant will use a bit further on, drawing on St Paul's language, one complies with the *letter* but not with the *spirit* of the law. But such compliance with the law is, for the perverse heart, only incidental and adds nothing in the way of moral worth. Depravity is worse than impurity, even though both can result in legal actions, precisely because at the level of impurity, one *intends* to act legally, whereas at the level of depravity, one intends to satisfy one's natural inclinations and only happens to act legally when doing so does not run counter to self-love.

Immediately after defining depravity, Kant writes: "It will be noted that the propensity to evil is here established (as regards actions) in the human being, even the best; and so it must also be if it is to be proved that the propensity to evil among human beings is universal, or, which here amounts to the same thing, that it is woven into human nature" (6:30). Kant clearly and unambiguously says here what has already been indicated in the title of Part I, that the propensity to evil—another way of designating the choice of an evil supreme maxim—is characteristic of human beings as a species, which is to say that every member of the human species subordinates the moral law to self-love from the very first use of his or her freedom. Kant says that this propensity to evil "is here established (as regards actions) in the human being, even the best." But *where* exactly is it established, and how? One finds a careful articulation of what it would mean to say that humans have a propensity to evil but no demonstration that humans *in fact do have a propensity to evil*. This curious remark has sent some Kant scholars on a hunt for this demonstration, assuming that it must be hiding somewhere in the text; other scholars have attempted to supply the missing proof themselves. We should note, though, that Kant says that this propensity to evil is here established "as regards actions"; it may be that Kant is claiming no more here than that a propensity to evil is demonstrated insofar as every human being, "even the best," has performed evil actions. Again, this is an empirical claim that it is impossible to demonstrate with complete certainty. Perhaps Kant thought it self-evident that because *everyone* performs evil deeds (a claim that he thought no one could reasonably object to), the basis was provided for the inference that there is a universal propensity to evil.

This reading is substantiated by Kant's claim in the following section that a "formal proof" of this propensity to evil in the human being is unnecessary, given the "multitude of woeful examples" of human deeds that our experience supplies us (6:32–33). Kant is certainly too impatient here to wait for the future anthropological research he mentions earlier! He proceeds in the rest of the paragraph to list the evil deeds of people who live in "the state of nature"—the place, he says, where a philosopher would most expect to encounter the natural goodness of humanity—as well as those of "civilized" peoples, who may not engage in the "ritual murders of Tofoa, New Zealand, and the Navigator Islands," but who are nevertheless guilty of other kinds of evil: "secret falsity even in the most intimate friendship," "a propensity to hate him to whom we are indebted," and a host of other vices often successfully "hidden under the appearance of virtue."

This, then, is a concise account of what I take to be the basis of Kant's claim that humans are evil by nature. While we cannot directly perceive maxims, nor the underlying supreme maxim or disposition, we can see actual deeds that are contrary to the law. And in most cases, in ourselves if not in others, we can make the inference from an evil deed to a particular evil maxim of action. Since the moral law allows no exceptions to its demand for the supremacy of the incentive of the moral law over the incentive of self-love, the presence of even one particular evil maxim can only result from a fundamental decision (the supreme maxim) to allow oneself to make an exception to the unconditional demands of the moral law—in other words, from an evil disposition. So, the question is: are evil deeds widespread enough, in different societies and at different times, to justify the claim that this evil disposition is universal? Kant thinks so. While it must be conceded that this does not amount to a definitive proof of the claim that humans are evil by nature, Kant was satisfied with it and confident that no one would really challenge this claim.

In addition, we should once again bear in mind the purpose of the *Religion*: to reinterpret Christian doctrine in light of morality. As we have seen, Kant's hermeneutic principles, as explicitly laid out in the *Conflict of the Faculties*, dictate that any dogma that does not interfere with morality the philosopher can leave alone, even if that dogma happens to make claims that transcend reason; however, if a dogma conflicts with moral principles, the philosopher *must* reinterpret that doctrine so that it becomes compatible with morality. Let's then think about these hermeneutic principles in relation to original sin. Kant does not have a problem with the idea that evil is universal, as the doctrine of original sin claims; he simply has a problem with the idea that this evil depends upon something other than our own freedom. So, rather than rejecting the doctrine of original sin altogether, Kant reinterprets it in a way that preserves the idea that evil is universal but insists on understanding this universal evil as the result of the free power of choice. To do this, he rather awkwardly stretches the meanings of words like "nature," "innate," and "propensity"; but by retaining these words, he preserves the language of original sin while making it compatible with morality. Having reinterpreted the words in this way, Kant is free to make the claim that humans are evil by nature, even if it cannot be proven with complete certainty that this claim is true. Religions make many claims that cannot be proven to be true; the important thing is that these claims do not interfere with the development of morality. Indeed, the self-scrutiny that would result from the idea that every human being without exception begins from an evil disposition is more beneficial, from a Kantian perspective, than an undeserved good conscience that might well result from believing himself or herself to be naturally good from birth.

Kant's reading of Genesis 2-3

We will end our analysis of Part I of the *Religion* by briefly considering Kant's philosophical interpretation of the story of the Fall of Adam and Eve in Genesis 2-3. The fact that Kant ends with scriptural interpretation drives home the point that one of his main objectives here is a hermeneutic neutralization of those elements of the doctrine of original sin that are a danger to morality. While Kant's reading of the Genesis story is perhaps not as fully developed as it might be, we can clearly see how he brings all of the previous argumentation to bear on the biblical account of the origin of evil.

In Section IV, Kant makes his first *direct* comment concerning the morally problematic nature of the orthodox doctrine of original sin.

He writes that whatever the original of moral evil in the human being might be, the most *inappropriate* way to represent the spread of this evil throughout the species is to represent it as having been inherited from our "first parents." If this is indeed how evil spreads, Kant says, then we can respond with Ovid: "Race and ancestors, and those things which we did not make ourselves, I scarcely consider as our own" (6:40). But if moral evil is not transmitted through inheritance from Adam and Eve, how precisely do we account for the origin of evil?

Before looking at the narrative of the Fall directly, Kant makes some important remarks concerning the idea of "origin." In the opening paragraph of Section IV, Kant defines origin (or the first origin) as "the descent of an effect from its first cause, i.e. from that cause which is not in turn the effect of another cause of the same kind" (6:39). This is clear enough; certainly when we inquire into the original of evil, we are asking about the first cause of a certain effect or effects. But Kant goes on to make a crucial distinction between origin "according to reason" and origin "according to time." Why does he introduce this distinction here?

Remember that for Kant, to be "in time" means to operate according to mechanical laws of causality. But the mechanical laws of causality are inimical to freedom, which is why Kant insists that the free will is noumenal, which is to say, outside of time. Free will must be a kind of causality that is free from the causality of the natural world. This is why Kant says here that it is a contradiction to search for the temporal origin of free actions, as though these free acts were simply natural effects (6:40). Now, the distinction between origin according to reason and origin according to time corresponds to the distinction between what originates in the free will (outside of time) and what originates in time in accordance with mechanical causal laws. Evil, Kant insists, cannot be the mechanical effect of the temporal state that precedes it—otherwise, evil wouldn't be the product of freedom and hence wouldn't be *evil* at all. Therefore, it makes no sense to speak of a *temporal* origin of evil.

For Kant, cause and effect in the natural world is such that if one were (perhaps like God) in a position to know every detail about the natural world at a given point in time, one could then predict with certainty what would occur at the following moment. This is because the natural world operates according to fixed mechanical laws. In other words, an event in the natural world is the mechanical effect of the state of the world that temporally precedes it. Such a picture of the world leaves little room for human freedom, which Kant insists is inimical to such natural causality. Kant, therefore, believes that the origin of moral evil—by which he means "the descent of an effect from its first cause"—cannot be merely the mechanical result of the preceding temporal state of affairs. If I am acting *freely*, then whatever state of affairs preceded my free action did not *determine* my action. In this sense, it would be improper to speak of my action as a temporal effect of the state of affairs of the natural world at the previous moment; insofar as I act freely, I act independently of such natural causality. Kant makes this point in what is certainly one of the more eloquent and important passages in Part I (6:41). He writes that whenever a human being performs an evil action, he must consider himself as having fallen into this evil directly from a state of innocence, since whatever his previous behavior might have been, this evil action was free and not causally determined. Therefore, the human being should have refrained from this evil action; and however evil he might have been in the past, acting morally "is still his duty *now*; he must therefore be capable of it and, should he not do it, he is at the moment of action just as accountable, and stands just as condemned, as if though endowed with a natural predisposition to the good (which is inseparable from freedom), he had just stepped out of the state of innocence into evil" (6:41). Thus, while the human being is certainly susceptible to the influence of natural causes, Kant insists that the human is still ultimately free and not determined by them, and therefore responsible for his actions in spite of such causal influences.

Kant's comment that we must consider "every evil action" as if the human being had "fallen into it directly from the state of innocence" is already a clue to how he will reinterpret the story of the Fall. As we have seen, evil cannot be constitutive of human nature in the ordinary sense—evil cannot be something we are literally born with—because humans are not responsible for the nature with which they are born. So, the fall into evil cannot be a single event that traces back to the origin of humanity from the first parents; in a certain sense, each of us must fall individually. And since, as Kant has just insisted, we remain free and responsible for our actions at every moment, independent of whatever state of affairs temporally precedes that moment, every evil action can, in a certain manner, be considered a fall from innocence. We must also note that for Kant, narratives are temporal by nature (they lay out a sequence of events); this means that when one narrates the origin of evil, there is the risk that this origin can be misunderstood as a temporal origin. And Kant has insisted that, properly speaking, there is no origin of evil according to time, only an origin of evil according to reason. Nevertheless, scripture presents the origin of evil in a narrative, and therefore temporal, form.

Kant begins the exegesis of Genesis in a rather peculiar way, because he seems to say precisely the opposite of what he has been arguing all along; he writes that evil begins *not* from a fundamental propensity to evil but from actual sin (transgression of the moral law considered as a divine commandment" (6:41–42). Kant's claim that evil cannot begin from a fundamental propensity to it seems to contradict the main argument of the book, that humans have a propensity to evil! But the contradiction disappears when we remind ourselves that for Kant, there are two ways to understand this word "propensity." If the human being is *born with* the propensity to evil, then it would not result from freedom. But if the human being somehow freely chooses this propensity itself, then evil can indeed be imputed to the human being. This is indeed how Kant redefines propensity, as we have seen, making it basically nothing other than the choice of a supreme evil maxim and therefore an evil disposition.

Kant will come to define "religion" in the *Religion* (and elsewhere) as the "recognition of one's duties as divine commands." We will have occasion to reflect in some detail over precisely what this definition means and entails. But for now, we should recall a point made in our discussion of the first edition Preface, that for Kant, God's commandments are nothing other than moral laws, and these commands are moral not *because God has commanded them*; rather, God has commanded them *because they are moral*. So, we can know the moral law independently of God and are ultimately responsible for upholding the moral law even if God does not exist. Nevertheless, we can consider the moral law as if it were a divine command. Human beings, for Kant, always experience the moral law as a command or *imperative* precisely because—as beings that are not purely rational, but *natural* as well, with inclinations and desires—humans are susceptible to incentives to act contrary to the moral law. This moral law commands us unconditionally (this is what Kant means by calling this imperative *categorical*).

And even though this command does not come from outside, we can nevertheless represent this command as if it were coming from a universal lawgiver—which, of course, sounds an awful lot like "God."

The idea that humans experience the moral law as a categorical imperative is represented in Genesis, says Kant, by God's command to Adam not to eat from the Tree of Knowledge of Good and Evil: "The moral law moved forward in the form of a *prohibition* (Gen. II.16-17), as befits a being who, like the human, is not pure but is tempted by inclinations" (6:42). It is important to note that while the prohibition God gives to Adam is a very specific command, on Kant's reading, this very specific prohibition stands for the moral law in general, experienced as a categorical imperative.

Instead of allowing the moral law to be a sufficient incentive, Adam searched out other incentives, making it his maxim to act in conformity with the law, not strictly out of duty but with regard to other incentives if need be (Gen. 3.6). If we go back to Kant's discussion of the three stages of the propensity to evil with this passage in mind, we see that this is precisely what Kant calls "impurity": the moral law does not serve as a sufficient incentive; there are other incentives, not good in themselves like the moral law, that aid in following one's duty. While this impurity may not yet constitute full-blown perversity, it is nevertheless the case that this adulteration of the moral law sets the stage for the subsequent "depravity" of the human being.

As a result of this initial adulteration of the moral law, Kant continues, the human being begins to question the stringency of the law, rationalizing the "downgrading" of his obedience to it to merely conditional obedience under the maxim of self-love. Then, as soon as the "sensory inducements" reach a critical mass, overriding the incentive of the moral law in the formation of a particular maxim of action, *sin*—an actual deed that transgresses the moral law—results. Thus, what begins as impurity turns into the incorporation of a nonmoral incentive into one's maxims, which, in turn, leads to the performance of an evil deed, eating the forbidden fruit. Just as God's command to Adam stands for the moral law generally, so too does Adam's Fall represent the fall of every human being, insofar as every human being has sinned. This is why Kant concludes, with Horace: *Mutato nomine de te fabula narratur*, "Change but the name, of you the tale is told" (6:42).

Kant's treatment of the serpent that tempts Eve is perhaps the most interesting facet of his interpretation of the biblical narrative. He remarks that, given our predisposition to the good, and given that evil does not derive from nature but from our free power of choice, it is inconceivable how moral evil could have arisen in us (6:43). Kant is quite sure of *what it means* to say that someone is evil, but why someone should *actually be evil*, given our predisposition to the good—that is a question to which Kant has no answer. And the incomprehensibility of this evil—the mystery of the question, "whence comes evil?"—is expressed in the biblical narrative "by projecting evil at the beginning of the world, not, however, with the human being, but in a *spirit* of an originally more sublime destiny" (ibid.). This "spirit of an originally more sublime destiny," of course, is Satan, whose evil nature is even more incomprehensible than the evil in human nature, precisely because as a spiritual rather than corporeal being, Satan does not experience inclinations that are contrary to the moral law in the way that human beings do. The biblical narrative projects the incomprehensible origin of evil onto Satan and understands the origin of human evil in terms of *temptation* rather than predisposition. Since the human being lapsed into evil through temptation, he is not fundamentally corrupt and therefore capable of moral improvement (6:44).

On this reading of scripture, not only is the ultimate incomprehensibility of evil affirmed, but also the human being remains responsible for his own evil (by succumbing to temptation). Moreover (and this is a crucial point), since human evil does not result from a *fundamental* corruption of the predisposition to the good, moral improvement always remains possible. This is the optimistic note upon which Kant ends the rather bleak Part I: there always remains the hope that the human being, however evil he might be, will return to the good (6:44).

Just as Christian theology is centered on God's actions to repair a fallen humanity, so is Kant's philosophical reinterpretation of the Christian doctrine of original sin followed by a philosophical reinterpretation of Christian teaching concerning the regeneration of the human being, both individually (Part II) and corporately, by means of the "church" (Part III). Before turning to Part II, however, we must briefly examine the important "General Remark" that follows Part I, the first of four such remarks, with one appended to each part of the *Religion*.

General Remark

We have a small textual issue to discuss here. At 6:44, Kant begins a new section, which he calls a "General Remark." Underneath the "General Remark," there is a descriptive title: "Concerning the restoration to its power of the original predisposition to the good." In the first edition of the *Religion*, as well as in the version of Part I published separately in the *Berlinische Monatsschrift*, the words "General Remark" do not appear; they were added only for the second edition. This might, on the surface, seem like an insignificant detail, but it may indeed impact one's interpretation of this section specifically and perhaps of the *Religion* as a whole. To see why I suggest this, the reader should jump to the final paragraph of this section, which begins at 6:52. This paragraph was added in the second edition (and is marked off—as are all of Kant's second edition additions—with a dagger). Kant begins this paragraph as follows: "This General Remark is the first of four which are appended, one to each Part of this writing, and which could bear the labels (1) Of Effects of Grace; (2) Miracles; (3) Mysteries; and (4) Means of Grace. – These are, as it were, *parerga* to religion within the boundaries of pure reason; they do not belong within it yet border on it." By assigning the title "General Remark" to the final section of Part I that begins at 6:44, rather than simply to this paragraph added to the second edition, Kant seems to suggest that the whole section could bear the title "Of Effects of Grace," and that this whole section does not belong to religion within the boundaries of pure reason, but rather borders on it. This is potentially significant for the interpretation of the *Religion* because, as we will see, most of what Kant says in this final section of the *Religion* he repeats in the main part (not the General Remark) of Part II. The implication would be that Part II, or at least some important discussions contained within it, is itself *parergonal*—bordering upon "religion within the boundaries of pure reason" but not properly a part of it. In other words, there is no clear demarcation of what lies "inside" pure reason and what is "outside" of it.

Before discussing the content of the "General Remark," let's look a bit more closely at what Kant means when he calls these remarks "parerga." *Parergon* is a Greek word that refers to a piece of work that is secondary or supplementary to the main work. So, in these

General Remarks, Kant is taking the liberty of straying outside of the confines of reason and therefore beyond the task he has set for himself: to analyze religion "within the boundaries of mere reason." But straying beyond the boundaries of mere reason, Kant seems to suggest, is inevitable: "Reason, conscious of its impotence to satisfy its moral needs, extends itself to extravagant ideas which might make up for this lack, though it is not suited to this enlarged domain" (6:52). This raises a few questions. (1) What exactly is this "impotence" of reason? (2) How do the four ideas addressed in the General Remarks try to compensate for this impotence? (3) Why is reason "not suited to this enlarged domain"?

The third question is the easiest to answer. In the very next sentence, Kant says that reason cannot dispute the possibility or even the actual existence of these ideas; it simply cannot incorporate these ideas into its maxims. Exactly like the idea of God, the ideas of grace, miracles, and mysteries transcend the limits of what humans can possibly know. Of course, just because humans cannot *know* whether they exist does not mean they *don't* exist. But whether or not they exist, the crucial point for Kant is that these ideas cannot be incorporated into the maxims—in other words, we must guard against, for example, allowing a belief in divine grace to unseat respect for the moral law as the ground of our maxims. Indeed, Kant says that each of these four ideas, when introduced into "religion" (read: of pure reason), produces four classes of corresponding ill effects: enthusiasm, superstition, illumination, and thaumaturgy. We will address these terms when discussing the *parerga* themselves. But the key idea here is that when venturing into the domain of grace, miracles, and mysteries, reason extends itself beyond its area of competence, risking the corruption of morality. If reason *needs* these *parerga* on account of its own impotence, it satisfies this need only by exposing itself to some measure of danger. Like a strong medicine, the power to heal is equally a power to poison.

The first question is rather more complex: why is reason "impotent" to satisfy its moral needs? This is a question that Kant does not directly address in this General Remark, though it is an issue that we discussed in connection to Kant's first edition Preface. While morality in itself has no need for the idea of God—and by extension, any transcendent religious ideas—it does not mean that religious ideas have no role to play in *human* morality. Humans are not purely rational beings, but also finite, sensible beings for whom happiness as the final *end* of action always remains in view. The idea of God, then, becomes necessary to guarantee the highest good—happiness in proportion to virtue—and therefore, morality leads to religion. But again, this is not because the moral law in itself does not stand firm on its own but because humans are not purely rational beings. This impotence of reason is only impotence in the face of *human finitude*.

Now, while the idea of God generated by practical reason is one that functions within the constraints imposed by morality, historical religion presents many equally transcendent ideas—like those of grace, mysteries, and miracles—that are not, strictly speaking, generated out of practical reason and therefore at least potentially pose a threat to it. Regarding these transcendent objects, Kant says that to have *dogmatic* faith—a faith that claims to be *knowledge*—appears to reason "dishonest or imprudent" (6:52). However, dogmatic faith is not the only stance one might take toward these ideas. There is also a *"reflective* faith"; this faith does not claim to be *knowledge*, since it only asserts the possibility of these objects. Nevertheless, reason "counts on this something being made available to its good will even if uncognized." The words "good will" here are crucial. For these ideas to be proper objects of a reflective faith, they must be subordinated to and put to the use of morality. The *parerga* to "religion within the boundaries of mere reason" are precisely those places in which reason can make use of these ideas, not with a dishonest "dogmatic faith" that claims to have knowledge of these transcendent objects but with a "reflective faith" that allows for the possibility of these objects, provided that they are put to moral use.

Our remaining question is: how it is that these transcendent ideas can be put to a moral use to satisfy the impotence of reason? Let's begin to answer this question by considering the transcendent idea under discussion in this first General Remark: the "effects of grace." (We will treat miracles, mysteries, and the means of grace as they arise later on in Parts II–IV.)

Recall our earlier observation that—given Kant's placement of the words "General Remark"—the entire final section of Part I concerns the "effects of grace." On the surface, this might not seem so obvious; after all, Kant does not use the word "grace" at all until that final paragraph added in the second edition. Nevertheless, Kant's concern in this entire final section of Part I is with the question of what

God does to assist us in becoming morally better human beings; and Kant defines the "effects of grace" as "supernatural moral influences to which we are merely passively related" (6:194)—in other words those things that God does for us to make us morally better without any contribution of our own. The various Christian doctrines concerning grace have a long and complex history that cannot be rehearsed here. But in the most general terms, we can say that, in the Christian tradition, "grace" is the gift of God's action in restoring the sinner to the good and making the sinner righteous in God's judgment. This grace is a gift insofar as it is unmerited (not earned through human actions). And God's grace is necessary because we cannot achieve salvation through our own effort on account of original sin. Therefore, it is hardly surprising that, having offered a moral reinterpretation of the doctrine of original sin, Kant would turn to the doctrine of grace, that through which the effects of original sin are undone.

As we have seen, Kant insists that the radical evil in human nature must be freely chosen for human beings to be responsible for it; in this sense, it cannot be "natural" in any usual sense of the term. For this evil to really be evil, it must be something that we have done for ourselves. It stands to reason, then, that for humans to become genuinely good, this too must be something they do for themselves. And this is exactly what we find Kant insisting in the opening sentence of the first General Remark: The human being must *make himself* into whatever he is in a moral sense, good or evil (6:44). But what does this mean for the idea of grace? If grace means that God makes us better instead of us making ourselves better, then for Kant, any improvement that comes through grace isn't really *moral* improvement. So, does Kant's approach to morality rule out any possibility of divine assistance in becoming morally good? If we understand grace to be entirely unmerited, or believe that without this grace, the human being couldn't do anything for the sake of becoming a better human being, then Kant's moral theory is certainly at odds with the idea of grace. But Kant does not simply dismiss the idea of grace altogether:

> Granted that some supernatural cooperation is also needed to his becoming good or better, whether this cooperation only consist in the diminution of obstacles or be also a positive assistance, the human being must nonetheless make himself antecedently

worthy of receiving it; and he must *accept* this help (which is no small matter), i.e. he must incorporate this positive increase of force into his maxim; in this way alone is it possible that the good be imputed to him, and that he be acknowledged a good human being. (6:44)

It is absolutely crucial here that Kant not be misunderstood to be conceding that supernatural cooperation *is* required; he is simply stipulating that *if* we were to grant (*concesso non dato*) that supernatural cooperation is needed, there are conditions that would have to be met in order for a human's improvement to be imputed to him: making himself worthy of this help and freely accepting this help. But what does it mean to make oneself "antecedently worthy" of receiving this help? Kant is extremely clear in this General Remark that the only thing one can do to make oneself worthy of this help is to become a better human being. Indeed, this marks the very fault line between moral religion—which Kant glosses as "the religion of *good life-conduct*"—and "religion of rogation" (religion of "mere cult") (6:51). All religions, Kant says, fall into one or other category. What is characteristic of religions of rogation is the belief that God can make the worshipper good—and therefore, eternally happy—without the worshipper himself having to do anything to make himself good, or at least nothing more than simply asking to be made good. Assuming that God is omniscient, all this "asking" really amounts to is "wishing"; and Kant adds that, if moral improvement required mere wishing, everyone would be morally good (which is certainly not the case). By contrast, it is a fundamental principle of moral religion that to become a better human being, one must do everything within one's power. Only then may one hope that what lies outside of one's power will be made good through supernatural cooperation (6:51–52). This does not amount to a claim that God actually does help those who do everything within their power; it is simply a claim concerning the conditions under which one can legitimately *hope* for such assistance.

Moreover, Kant is clear in this General Remark that it is not necessary for human beings to have knowledge of what God has done or will do for them; it is only necessary for the human being to know what he himself must do to become *worthy* of divine assistance (6:52). In fact, it is impossible to ever know what, if anything, God has done for us in this respect. As Kant notes at the very end of this

General Remark, if we are keeping reason within its proper limits, our concepts of cause and effect can only be applied to what lies within the natural order—this is one of the basic insights of the first *Critique*. But to talk about what God has done for us is to apply causality to something (God) that lies outside of the natural order. We cannot claim to have experienced the effects of grace without falling into *enthusiasm*—a kind of dangerous religious fervor that derives from believing oneself to be the recipient of an inner experience or illumination (more on this point below). Nor, Kant says, can we really make any practical employment of the idea of an effect of grace without falling into contradiction. This is because practical reason involves formulating principles concerning what one must *do* to achieve a particular end. But the very idea of an effect of grace means that the good that is brought about by this divine action is not our own doing. So, we cannot incorporate it into our own maxims of action, even if we admit this grace as theoretically possible.

If there is any place left for grace in Kant, it is so carefully circumscribed as to be at odds with many if not most Christian doctrines of grace. Kant doesn't deny the theoretical possibility of grace—he cannot do so without claiming to know something that by his own standards he couldn't possibly know—though he is very careful to ensure that the idea of grace does not undermine morality, through his insistence that the *sine qua non* of any divine assistance in our moral progress be our own efforts at moral improvement. And yet, if moral worth is linked to what we ourselves do of our own power, it is not at all clear how it would be possible for God to contribute to the effort anyway. We will return to this problem in Part II, since this General Remark is not Kant's last word on grace.

Kant makes some important points in this General Remark that we have not touched on (6:45–6:51). However, these points anticipate issues that will be discussed again and more fully in Part II. Therefore, we will defer comment on them until then and close our discussion with a comment about "enthusiasm." When these four objects discussed in the four General Remarks are the objects of a dogmatic rather than a reflective faith and are, therefore, not subordinated to morality, there are potentially dangerous results. Corresponding to each of the transcendent ideas that are the subjects of the four General Remarks—"effects of grace," "miracles," "mysteries," and "means of grace"—are four attendant dangers: enthusiasm, superstition, illumination, and thaumaturgy. These, Kant says, represent "aberrations" of a reason that has strayed beyond its proper limits (6:52–53).

The danger, then, that corresponds to a dogmatic belief in the effects of grace is "enthusiasm" (*Schwärmerei*). While Kant does not fully expound upon the meaning of this term here, he does gloss it as a "*supposed* inner experience" (my italics) in the passage quoted above. Later, in Part IV, Kant writes that pretending to experience these effects of grace is "an enthusiastic delusion pertaining merely to feeling" (6:194). Ultimately, what makes such inner experience delusional is that one claims to have experienced an intuition of something supernatural, for which the human being possesses no appropriate sense faculty (see 6:175).

Why such enthusiasm is dangerous might not be evident from Kant's mention of it in this General Remark. But James DiCenso notes that "Kant follows an established tradition of critical thinking about the dangers of enthusiasm," a tradition that includes Locke, Spinoza, and Hume (2011, 39). And these dangers include, for Kant, fanaticism and even the destruction of freedom of thought, a point that Kant makes in his 1786 essay, "What Does It Mean to Orient Oneself in Thinking" (see 8:145). We will return to these issues in our analysis of Part IV of the *Religion*, where Kant discusses in detail the dangers of religious delusion and "counterfeit" religion.

Part II: Concerning the battle of the good against the evil principle for dominion over the human being

Part I of the *Religion* purports to establish that humans begin from a position of radical evil. Kant has not, in fact, proven this point; but this hardly matters, as I have argued. Through his formulation of the radical evil of human nature, Kant neutralizes the morally dangerous elements of the Christian doctrine of original sin, while retaining those elements of the doctrine that are useful from a practical point of view. Indeed, the assumption that humans begin from a position of radical evil may be quite useful, insofar as it leads one away from the complacency of an undeserved good conscience, which may result from believing oneself to be good from birth, and toward the self-scrutiny that ethical life demands.

I also noted that while Kant's thesis concerning radical evil sounds pessimistic, it is, in fact, optimistic, precisely because this evil results from free choice and can, therefore, be freely overcome. This is not to say that overcoming evil is easy; the title of Part II indicates that this process is a "battle of the good against the evil principle for dominion over the human being." If this sounds rather apocalyptic, that's precisely the point: Kant is going to interpret the religious representations of the struggle between good and evil in terms of the change from an evil to a good disposition.

Before addressing Christian representations of the struggle between good and evil, Kant begins Part II with some comments on the Stoics. The Stoics, according to Kant, correctly perceived that the human being must *actively* struggle against evil, for which virtue, meaning strength or valor, is required; but they mistook the natural inclinations for the enemy. Kant already argued in Part I that the natural inclinations cannot be the source of moral evil; evil is rooted instead in the freely chosen maxim to follow those inclinations when they run counter to morality. In a footnote to these opening remarks in Part II, Kant says that the inclinations only make the execution of good maxims more difficult; genuine evil, however, is located squarely in the *will* not to oppose these inclinations (6:59n).

If the Stoics fail to properly identify the true cause of evil, it is because evil is inexplicable. This is not to say that Kant is unsure what evil is or where it resides; Kant is entirely certain that evil is located in the freely chosen supreme maxim. But the ultimate origin of evil cannot be explained, precisely because morality itself is a mystery. I will refer to this thesis, that the origin of morality—and correspondingly, the origin of moral transgression—cannot ultimately be explained or accounted for, as the "Mystery of Morality" (MoM) thesis. Why exactly does Kant think that morality is a mystery?

That human action should be governed by instinct and aim at the fulfillment of the natural inclinations would hardly seem surprising; everywhere we look, we see other, nonhuman animals acting instinctively and ineluctably for the sake of satisfying their natural inclinations. There is nothing moral or immoral about this, precisely because this animal instinct is a natural mechanism. As we learned in Part I, there is also a predisposition to humanity that sets us apart from the rest of the animal kingdom. This predisposition, which results from the human capacity to compare oneself with others, is utilized by nature for the development of culture. But ultimately, this predisposition to humanity is, like the predisposition to animality, natural and therefore amoral, so long as the predisposition to *personality* is not present. It is only when the predisposition to personality—the susceptibility of the human being to experience the moral law as a sufficient incentive to determine the power of choice—is taken into account that we can begin to speak of moral good and evil. Because of this predisposition to personality, the human being breaks free from the stranglehold of nature and responds to the call of the moral law, even when this law demands that we repress our instincts and sacrifice the fulfillment of our natural inclinations. *How* it is, however, that human beings, alone in the animal kingdom, should become capable of subordinating every other incentive and making respect for the moral law its own incentive—this, Kant says, is "absolutely inexplicable" (6:59n). In Part I, Kant already expressed his wonder at this moral predisposition by which we are elevated far above nature; its very incomprehensibility, Kant says, proclaims a "divine origin" (6:49–50). But beyond merely expressing wonder and astonishment at our moral predisposition, Part I gives a philosophical account of the inexplicability of morality. Recall his distinction between an "origin according to reason" and an "origin according to time" (6:39). Why are humans capable of being good? When we ask for an explanation of why something is the case, we are generally asking for an account of the origin of that thing. Insofar as moral good is the product of freedom, it cannot be given a causal explanation or assigned an "origin according to time," precisely because the free will, for Kant, is not "in time." We cannot find a causal explanation for moral good as we can for natural phenomena. All we can say about moral good is that it has an "origin according to reason," which is simply to say that it originates in freedom. To look for a further explanation would be to try to find a causal explanation for freedom, something that for Kant would be a contradiction in terms, since to be free means to be free of causal determination.

But the corollary to the inexplicability of the predisposition to the good is the inexplicability of evil; for just as it is inconceivable how the moral law alone could overpower the force of nature, it is also incomprehensible how the natural inclinations could overpower reason, which commands with such "authority." The cause of human evil, therefore, "remains forever shrouded in darkness" (6:59). This is why Kant thinks of moral good and moral evil as ultimately inexplicable. Kant will make use of this MoM thesis at a number of junctures in the *Religion*.

Recall that at the end of Part I, Kant says that the Bible expressed the incomprehensibility of evil by projecting its origin onto Satan, who induces evil in humans through temptation. Kant sounded a note of hope there: because humans lapsed into evil through temptation and not through a fundamentally corrupt nature, there is hope for their restoration to the good. But the fact that humans were tempted does not ultimately mitigate their guilt. In the final paragraph preceding Section One of Part II, Kant notes that Paul (the "apostle") represents the invisible enemy against which humans must strive as an evil spirit that exists outside of us (Kant is referring here to Eph. 6:12). On the surface, this seems not to fit with Kant's ethical theory, which locates evil squarely in the human will. But Kant doesn't balk at this representation, for two reasons. First, Paul is simply trying "to make intuitive, *for practical use*, the concept of something to us unfathomable" (6:59): scripture should not be taken as trying to make any transcendent claims; it is simply illustrating the incomprehensibility of evil by representing this evil in the form of an external spirit. Second, it makes no difference from a practical perspective whether this enemy is inside or outside, since we are equally guilty either way; we could not be tempted were we not "in secret agreement" with the tempter (6:60). So, while our temptation is a source of consolation in Part I (because it shows that we are not fundamentally corrupt), here in Part II, the fact that we are susceptible to temptation means that the Satan we are combating is to be found right inside of us.

Section One: Concerning the rightful claim of the good principle to dominion over the human being

A The personified idea of the good principle

If you know the Bible well, or at least if you follow the translator's notes to this section, you will see that Kant has tightly woven together a number of scriptural passages about Jesus, most of which come from the Gospel of John. This gospel, particularly its prologue (Jn 1.1-18, "In the beginning was the Word . . ."), has the most sophisticated and exalted conception of Jesus' identity and is, therefore, central to the subsequent development of the branch of Christian theology known as "Christology," which concerns the nature and person of Jesus Christ. In this section, Kant translates a number of scriptural passages about Jesus Christ into his own practical idiom; to this extent one might say that he offers his own Christology. It is very different from the Christology produced by the ecumenical councils of the early church, which became normative for the Catholic Church and most Protestant denominations, including Lutheranism. Yet to say that Kant offers a new Christology is not entirely accurate, since Christology in its usual sense concerns realities that transcend the limits of human knowledge. Kant's "Christology" does not really represent a speculation concerning the nature of Christ, but rather a repurposing of Christological language to make it conform to moral religion.

Kant's basic interpretive strategy can be briefly characterized as follows: Kant reads the Jesus of scripture as an ideal of human moral perfection, or in other words, as a concrete representation of an individual being who is adequate to the idea of moral perfection. Of course, the idea of moral perfection that Kant is working with is the idea of a will that is *always* determined by the moral law rather than self-love, no matter how many temptations to the contrary he is subjected to. Insofar as this ideal is presented to us as a model to be emulated, Jesus constitutes a "prototype" (*Urbild*) of human moral perfection. However, this ideal of moral perfection is one that practical reason generates all by itself; we do not need scripture to teach us what this ideal is, as Kant will argue. Nevertheless, such an ideal can play a positive role in the cultivation of morality, as we will see.

If one keeps in mind that, for Kant, the Jesus of the gospels is simply a concrete representation of an individual being adequate to the idea of moral perfection, then one can understand a feature of the *Religion* that is otherwise quite puzzling: Kant almost never refers to Jesus by name. The gospels, on Kant's reading, portray an individual being that represents the idea of moral perfection. Whether or not this being actually existed as a historical person is beside the point, for two reasons. First, an ideal does not have to exist to function as an ideal. Indeed, insofar as ideals are generated by practical reason and not derived from existing things, ideals are fictions. As the title of this section indicates, Kant's concern here is with a personified moral idea, not with a historical being. Second, even if the historical Jesus were a living embodiment of a morally perfect human being as scripture portrays him, there would be no way for us to know this; after all, Jesus' disposition is no more open to human inspection than anyone else's. I would go so far as to say that for Kant, even if it turns out that Jesus never existed, or at least never was entirely what a literal reading of scripture makes him out to be, this would not in itself undermine the validity or usefulness of the gospel narratives as a portrayal of the prototype of moral perfection.

The prologue to the Gospel of John (1.1-18), as I said, contains some of the most exalted statements about Jesus Christ. The author of this gospel speaks of Jesus as a "Word" (*logos*) through which God created the world, evoking the opening lines of the creation account in Genesis, where God creates by means of his verbal command, "Let there be . . ." This Word preexists creation and is in some sense identical to God. In the opening paragraph of Section One, Kant begins to interpret these ideas through his ethical lens. He starts with the idea that "*Humanity . . . in its full moral perfection*" represents the purpose for which God created the world (6:60). Naturally, the happiness of human beings would follow from this moral perfection, since Kant's idea of God is the idea of a moral author of the world that wills the happiness of human beings in proportion to their worthiness of receiving it. Since the morally perfect human being is the reason for which God created the world, we can say that this human being "is in him from eternity" (cf. Jn 1.1-2); and since this idea "proceeds from God's being," we can say that this idea is not a part of the created world, but rather "God's only begotten Son, 'the Word' (the *Fiat!*) through which all other things are, and without whom nothing that is made would exist" (cf. Jn 1.3). Nothing would exist were it not for this idea of human moral perfection because, as Kant already stated, humanity in its full moral perfection represents the very purpose for which God created the world. Human beings can fulfill this purpose and become "children of God" (cf. Jn 1.12) through the adoption of the dispositions of this ideal of moral perfection (6:60–61). Kant may be playing fast and loose with scriptural language here, but his goal is clear: to read the subject matter of John's prologue as concerning the ideal of human moral perfection rather than a transcendent, divine, or semidivine being.

As moral beings, we generate this ideal of a human being in its full moral perfection, and therefore, we have a duty to "elevate ourselves" to it—in other words, to make this ideal a "prototype" for ourselves. Kant once again draws on the MoM thesis when he claims that we are not the "authors" of this ideal of moral perfection, but that this idea has "established itself" in the human being without us understanding how we could be receptive of it (6:61). Because we cannot understand how humanity could be receptive to this idea, we can say that this prototype has come down from heaven (6:61). In this way, Kant appropriates the biblical language that suggests—and the Christian dogma that claims—that God assumed human form in the person of Jesus Christ.

The suffering and persecution of Jesus, documented in the "passion narratives" of the gospels, represents the idea that a human being in his moral perfection is willing to take upon himself all manner of suffering for the sake of the good principle (6:61). Such suffering might involve the sacrifice of one's natural instincts where they conflict with the moral law (resisting temptation, as Jesus resists Satan's temptations in the wilderness after his baptism) or the suffering that comes with a principled stand on the side of the good. Jesus' persecution and crucifixion for his teachings—which, Kant will show later, are essentially moral teachings—are the inevitable result of the fact that the prototype of moral perfection dwells in a world where evil is abundant, if not omnipresent.

Finally, Christian theology stresses the salvific power of faith in Jesus Christ. Kant will say much more about whether and how Jesus plays a role in our salvation. But for now, we should note that Kant translates the saving power of faith in the prototype of a humanity well-pleasing to God in the following way: a human must have a "practical faith" in this prototype of the morally perfect human, which is to say, he must be "conscious of such a moral disposition in himself as enables him to *believe* and self-assuredly trust that he, under similar temptations and afflictions . . . would steadfastly cling to the prototype of humanity and follow this prototype's example in loyal emulation" (6:62). In other words, the human being must have faith not in the saving power of another human being (Jesus) but in his own ability to live up to this moral ideal. This is the only sort of "faith in the Son of God" that makes a human "not an unworthy object of divine pleasure" (ibid.).

B The objective reality of this idea

This idea of humanity in its moral perfection is produced by our morally legislative reason. Invoking his "ought implies can" principle, Kant says that it must be possible for us to conform to this idea, since it is clear to every reflecting human being that he ought to do so. Kant claims that he does not have to provide a proof that it is *possible* to conform to this idea; indeed, if one were to require that Kant first prove the possibility of what we ought to do, then he would have to prove that it is possible for us to uphold the moral law. But such a demonstration wouldn't be possible. Remember that Kant has insisted (the MoM thesis) that we *cannot know how* it is possible that the moral law furnishes a stronger incentive than the incentives of the natural inclinations; nevertheless, Kant would say, all human beings experience the authority of the moral law, even when they choose self-love over the moral law. So, we are not going to have any success, according to Kant, demonstrating the possibility of the moral law.

But what if we had an *example* of a human being choosing the moral law over self-love? Couldn't we then say that it is possible for humans to act morally, because a human being *actually did* act morally? The problem here is that we can never be entirely sure that any human being actually is acting morally, thus furnishing an example of the moral law, because the underlying dispositions cannot be seen. Kant makes this point clear in the *Groundwork*, where he writes that one "cannot show with certainty in any example that the will is here determined merely through the law, without another incentive, although it seems to be so" (4:419). So, we cannot prove that it is possible for us to conform to this idea of moral perfection through examples. The best one can do is to make oneself into an example of this moral idea; it is what the moral law requires us to do, after all (6:63). Of course, Kant has his own doubts that a human can ever be completely certain of his own moral disposition and thus act as his own example; his own self-observation cannot give him an "entirely reliable cognition" of the ground of his maxims or of the purity and stability of these maxims (6:63). But Kant is careful to note that even if there has never yet been an example of human moral perfection, the duty to conform to it is in no way undermined.

What bearing does Kant's point concerning moral examples have on the philosophical interpretation of Jesus? First of all, it means that it wouldn't be possible for Jesus to provide an example of moral perfection, since moral perfection can never be known by way of examples. This does not imply, however, that one cannot use examples for the purpose of moral education and to help bring to awareness and conscious reflection moral principles that are already present in reason. Indeed, the whole of the *Religion* is predicated on the idea that even though historical religion (with its symbols, representations, narratives, etc.) is not strictly necessary for ethics and rational religion, it nevertheless can play an important role in the moral progress of human beings, precisely because they are not purely rational creatures but sensible as well. Kant will remark in Part III that there is a "natural need of all human beings to demand for even the highest concepts and grounds of reason something that *the senses can hold on to*, some confirmation from experience or the like" (6:109). Second, even if Jesus, or any other human being, could serve as an example of moral perfection, we would need to be *already in possession* of this idea in order to recognize Jesus as an example of moral perfection. As Kant famously writes in the *Groundwork*: "Even the Holy One of the Gospel must first be compared with our ideal of moral perfection before he is cognized as such" (4:408). The conclusion, then, is that we cannot demonstrate the objective reality of this idea of moral perfection, since we cannot explain how it is that the mere idea of conformity to the law can be sufficient to determine the power of choice, and since we cannot provide an actual example of conformity to this idea of moral perfection.

Kant has an additional worry about Christian teachings concerning Jesus in this section. Traditional Christian belief, as I noted, represents Jesus as the fully human yet fully divine incarnation of God. As with all transcendent dogmas, Kant notes that we cannot know that this claim is true (since it transcends human experience), though at the same time we cannot deny the possibility of a supernaturally begotten human (6:63). Kant's real interest, however, is with the practical import of this speculative claim. His conclusion is that, from a practical point of view, Jesus' divine origin "is of no benefit to us," since the ideal of perfection that Jesus represents must be in us natural human beings as well. Whatever divinity Jesus might happen to possess is irrelevant to the ideal of moral perfection that we mere humans are obligated to emulate. In fact, divinizing Jesus undermines his ability to serve as a moral example. The "elevation of such a Holy One above every frailty of human nature" would put too great a distance between Jesus and every other human being for him to serve as an example for human imitation (6:64). While Kant does not come out and say that Jesus was simply a human being and not divine—a point about which Kant must remain agnostic—he clearly claims that asserting Jesus' divinity undercuts his efficacy as an example for emulation. Since morality is the *raison d'être* of religion, for Kant, the philosophical interpreter of religion must necessarily downplay the divinity of Jesus, even if he cannot altogether deny it.

Before moving on to the next section, let's make one final note, on the subject of miracles (about which Kant will say more in the General Remark to Part II). Jesus performs many miracles in the gospels and many miracles are woven into the narrative of his life, from the virgin birth to his resurrection from death. Miracles in the New Testament in particular, and in the Bible more broadly, serve first and foremost to demonstrate authority. They show that the person in question (usually some sort of prophet) is, in fact, God's genuine representative and that God's power is working through him. And in Jesus' case, the miracles are taken to confirm his supernatural identity. But Kant's Jesus is first and foremost a prototype of a human perfection, and since this prototype derives from reason, miracles are unnecessary to establish its authority as a model for us to emulate. All that is needed to accept Jesus or any other human as a prototype of human perfection is "a course of life entirely blameless and as meritorious as indeed one may ever wish." To demand more than this—to demand miracles, as well, to establish the authority of this prototype—is to confess to one's "own moral *unbelief*, to a lack of faith in virtue which no faith based on miracles . . . can remedy" (6:62–63).

C Difficulties that stand in the way of the reality of this idea, and their solution

As Kant's title to this section states, he is going to address and resolve several difficulties that stand in the way of our emulating the idea of a morally perfect humanity. We will consider these difficulties and their resolutions in order.

Difficulty 1
According to Kant, the moral law commands us to holiness. Loosely quoting Jesus' words in Matthew 5.48, Kant writes that the ideal set before us by this "Son of God" (prototype of human moral perfection) is to be holy in the conduct of our lives just as our "Father in Heaven" is holy (6:66). But what exactly does "holiness" mean here? It is important to be precise, because Kant uses this word in more than one sense. For example, in the *Groundwork*, Kant contrasts a holy will—which is to say, a purely rational will *incapable* of acting contrary to duty—with the finite rational will of human beings (see 4:414). Human beings do experience incentives to act contrary to the moral law, which is why they experience the moral law in the form of a command or categorical imperative. But because God, for example, does not have a sensible nature and therefore experiences no natural inclinations to rival the moral law, God cannot possibly violate the moral law. Thus, we can't call God "virtuous," since virtue presupposes a conflict between moral and nonmoral incentives. For God, there is no possibility of conflict; he is purely rational and therefore acts in accordance with the moral law automatically and ineluctably; God possesses a "holy will." But this kind of holiness—one characteristic of a divine being—is not the holiness to which humans are commanded here in the *Religion*, for the simple reason that this kind of holiness is *not possible* for beings that are both sensible and rational.

It seems that Kant's thought underwent some evolution with regard to the idea of holiness. In the second *Critique*, he argues that we are justified in postulating the immortality of the soul because the moral law demands holiness, which is a "perfection of which no rational being of the sensible world is capable at any moment of his existence" (5:122). Therefore, we must assume endless progress toward this holiness, which presupposes the immortality of the soul. It is not clear how exactly this immortality brings us closer to a holiness of which we are never capable without altogether ceasing to be sensible beings. In any case, the point is that holiness is, in the second *Critique*, not possible for us in this life. In his lectures on ethics, Kant discusses Jesus as a prototype of holiness. But there he defines holiness as "that state of mind from which an evil desire never arises" (29:604), something that is clearly not possible for sensible beings.

In the *Religion*, Kant leaves this understanding of Jesus' holiness behind. Instead, holiness in the *Religion* refers to the moral perfection consisting in always prioritizing the moral law over competing incentives. In fact, in Section B, as we have seen, Kant insists that the prototype of moral perfection should not be "above every frailty of human nature" and that this prototype must experience the same natural inclinations and temptations to transgression that we do (6:64); otherwise, this prototype could not be a model for human emulation. So, we are not commanded to have a perfectly holy will that never experiences any temptation. We are simply commanded to resist whatever temptations we encounter. The *Religion* presents us with a much more human model of human perfection. Since this is a perfection of which we must be capable, it is not surprising that the second *Critique*'s idea of immortality—which was necessitated in the first place by the impossibility of a sensible being to be holy—plays almost no role in the *Religion*.

But let's return to the difficulty at hand. Kant says that the moral law commands us to be holy, and as I have argued, this is a holiness of which we must be capable. So where, exactly, is the difficulty? It lies in the fact that even though we are commanded to holiness, we nevertheless constantly judge ourselves as falling short of this holiness. Why should we constantly judge ourselves as falling short, if indeed this holiness is something of which we are capable?

The important distinction to keep in mind here is the difference between *actually* falling short of holiness and simply *believing oneself* to have fallen short of holiness. The problem that Kant is dealing with in this first difficulty (and in the second one, as we will see) is essentially an *epistemological* problem. In explaining this epistemological problem, I will supplement Kant's remarks here in Part II with what he says in the first General Remark, which, as noted earlier, anticipates this discussion.

First of all, we know that a disposition is either good or evil; there is no middle ground. Therefore, the change from evil to good, on the level of the disposition, is a kind of "revolution": as Kant writes, that a human should become not merely *legally* good, but also *morally* good, "cannot be effected through gradual *reform* but must rather be effected through a *revolution* in the disposition of the human being (a transition to the maxim of holiness of disposition)" (6:47). But the human being cannot directly know that this revolution of disposition has taken place. The disposition, as the free ground of maxims, is nontemporal and therefore cannot be perceived by humans, who can only perceive things temporally. This means that human beings know this nontemporal revolution only by its temporal effects, which take the form of a gradual progress from bad to better, in a process of "incessant laboring and becoming" (6:48). Because the human being experiences this revolution of disposition as a gradual reformation, he always finds himself inadequate to the holiness of disposition to which he is commanded, even if he does, in fact, have a holy disposition.

Kant's solution to this problem, insofar as it stands in need of a solution, is simply to remind the reader that God judges on the basis of the disposition, not the deed. Since we must judge on the basis of the deed, we feel ourselves to be inadequate to the holiness of the moral law. But since God "scrutinizes the heart"—that is, the disposition—"through his pure intellectual intuition," he sees the disposition not in a state of becoming but as a perfect and completed whole. Therefore, whenever the human being should die, even though he feels himself to have fallen short of the ideal to which he is commanded, he will nevertheless be found to be pleasing to God (6:67). Immortality is not required to live up to the demands of the moral law.

Difficulty 2

The second difficulty that Kant addresses concerns the "moral happiness" of the person seeking to emulate the prototype of human moral perfection. Kant distinguishes between moral happiness and physical happiness. Physical happiness involves "contentment in one's *physical state* (freedom from evils and the enjoyment of ever mounting pleasures)." Moral happiness, on the other hand, consists in "the assurance of the reality and *constancy* of a disposition that always advances in goodness (and never falters from it)" (6:67). Note that there are two different issues here: assurance of the reality of the disposition, or assurance that one has a good disposition in the first place; and assurance of the constancy of the disposition, or assurance that one will persevere in this good disposition and not slide back into evil.

Both kinds of assurance present a problem. Since we only see deeds and not the disposition, not even our own, it seems that we can never be assured of the reality of the good disposition. And even if we could have such assurance, we lack the ability to see into the future, so it is unclear how we could be assured of the constancy of this disposition. After all, if a human can freely undergo a revolution from a bad disposition to a good one, there is no reason to think that a human can't revert to evil.

One might well ask Kant: Why is assurance important anyway? Even if we can't have any assurance of the present or future goodness of our disposition, the moral law still commands us unconditionally to become good. How does our inability to *know* how we are progressing pose a problem? Strictly speaking, assurance isn't necessary. Yet Kant is concerned with the issue for two reasons. First, while the unconditionally binding nature of the moral law does not hinge on the possibility of moral happiness, moral happiness is nevertheless important to moral beings. The inability to have any degree of assurance in the goodness and constancy of one's disposition can, therefore, serve as an impediment to moral progress. As Kant comments: "without *any* confidence in the disposition once acquired, perseverance in it would hardly be possible" (6:68). (Of course, too much assurance might well have pitfalls, too.) Second, the issue of assurance of salvation is a Christian theological issue. Like many other theological issues, Kant seeks to render it amenable to morality.

We can distinguish between the *ontological* question of salvation, which is the question of how one is saved, and the *epistemological* question of salvation, or the question of how one knows that one is saved.[1] In broad terms, Kant's ontology of salvation is a simple one: one finds favor with God through a moral life alone. But as we will see shortly in Difficulty 3, assuming that one starts from a place of radical evil, there is still a problem with salvation, namely how one can pay the debt of sin that one has incurred through the evil disposition. This second difficulty, meanwhile, is exclusively concerned with the *epistemology* of salvation. Granted that the only thing that pleases God is a good disposition, two questions remain: how can one know

---

[1] I am taking this distinction from Keith D. Stanglin's *Arminius on the Assurance of Salvation: The Context, Roots, and Shape of the Leiden Debate, 1603–1609* (Leiden: Brill, 2007). Stanglin provides a helpful overview of the history of the theological problem of assurance; see pp. 152–73.

whether one has a good disposition and how can one know that one will persevere in this good disposition?

One of the central texts in the discussion of the doctrine of assurance is Romans 8.16: "The Spirit itself beareth witness with our spirit, that we are the children of God." Kant takes this text to mean that whoever possesses a pure disposition will feel himself to be incapable of lapsing back into evil. But Kant is clearly suspicious of this idea and of all feelings presumed to be of a supernatural origin, for "one is never more easily deceived than in what promotes a good opinion of oneself" (6:68). Rather than encouraging confidence in one's good disposition, it is more beneficial to "work out one's salvation with fear and trembling" (Phil. 2.12). Yet this anxiety-laden position, Kant says, can also "drive one to the darkest enthusiasm" (6:68). It is not altogether clear what Kant means by this; perhaps he is referring to a presumed feeling, of supernatural origin, that one is not saved but damned. In any case, if we imagine a sliding scale of assurance, with total assurance at one end and complete lack of assurance at the other, we could say that Kant wants to stake out a position somewhere in the middle: a position of confidence in the disposition that does not cross over into "the sweetness or anxiety of enthusiasm" (6:68).

Kant's solution to the problem of assurance is a rather simple one. The person in question should consider his life from the time at which he committed himself to adopt a good way of life. Has he observed a steady improvement in the conduct of his life? If so, then he has reason to infer an improved disposition and reason to hope that he will persevere in his present course, even if his life were to extend beyond this one. This rational hope stems from the fact that any advance in the good always increases one's strength for future advances. Therefore, our assurance stems not from any supernatural experience but from our own awareness (such as it is) of our good disposition, as manifested through good life conduct. The moral life, then, brings its own assurance (6:70–71). However, should this person see no improvement in his conduct despite his resolution to be good, he has reason to regard his corruption as rooted in his disposition and little reason to hope for improvement, even in a future life.

Difficulty 3
The third difficulty is that even if one acquires a good disposition and perseveres in the good, one nevertheless started from evil—an

evil constituting a debt that cannot be erased. Therefore, it seems that despite this moral improvement, one will still be found lacking in righteousness when judged by God. Being made righteous in God's eyes (a theological problem known as the problem of *justification*) seems to require some means of atonement by which this debt of sin can be paid.

Traditional Christian theology places Jesus' death and resurrection at the center of the process of atonement. There are many different models for conceptualizing precisely how this atonement is brought about. In the Protestant tradition relevant for Kant, Jesus is thought to suffer the punishment for sin on our behalf, which he can do because he himself is without sin. As you might expect, this idea of atonement is a problem for Kant; any acceptable idea of atonement will have to be linked directly to what a person does *for himself* in a moral sense, not what another does for him as he sits idly by.

Regarding the human being's debt of sin, Kant makes several points: (1) even if someone who has undergone a change of disposition has not incurred new sins, his previous sins are not canceled; (2) doing good cannot produce a "surplus" to pay off the old debt, because doing good is what we are obligated to do anyway; and (3) this debt cannot be paid off by another person, since moral debts are not transferable in the way that financial debts are. This third point is the most radical with respect to orthodox Christian theology, as it directly contradicts the idea that Jesus' actions can result in atonement for the sins of others. Kant writes that the debt of sin is "the *most personal* of all liabilities, namely a debt which only the culprit, not the innocent, can bear, however magnanimous the innocent might be in wanting to take the debt upon himself for the other" (6:72). Finally, Kant notes (4) that the previously evil disposition results in an "infinity" of violations of the law and therefore produce infinite guilt. While a particular evil deed is a finite violation of the law, the choice of an evil disposition, as we know, is not simply one deed among others, but rather an original, radical perversion of the incentives of action. As Kant says, it is not an individual transgression but a perversion of the maxims in general. Therefore, the guilty party must expect "*infinite* punishment and exclusion from the Kingdom of God" (ibid.).

So, how can atonement take place? According to Kant's strictures, the human being must somehow make the atonement himself.

Yet future good behavior alone is not sufficient to do it. To solve this problem, Kant makes extensive use of scriptural language, specifically that of Paul's letters. In this way, Kant constructs an account of atonement that will seem biblical, even as it is fundamentally at odds with the traditional Protestant doctrine of atonement.

Kant asks whether punishment, which is the consequence of a previous evil disposition, should be applied to the human being in his new, morally converted state. On the one hand, any punishment the human being might have received prior to his moral conversion cannot be thought of as fully exacted, since, as Kant previously argued, the evil human being deserves infinite punishment. And yet, such infinite punishment seems hardly appropriate for the postconversion "new man." Can't God just decide to *forgive* the previous debt of sin? That would certainly be an easy solution. But Kant doesn't see this as a possibility; justice requires that satisfaction be made, and God, as a supremely just judge, can allow no sin to go unpunished (6:73). This might sound a little, well, unforgiving, but in defense of Kant's view, we should keep two points in mind. First, Christian theologians by and large make the same point, that God's justice demands that satisfaction be rendered. After all, if God could just forgive without the need for satisfaction, then Jesus' atoning sacrifice seems rather gratuitous. Second, we should recall why, according to Kant, the idea of God arises out of practical reason in the first place: to proportion the happiness of the human being precisely with his worthiness of receiving it ("virtue"). God is the exacting dispenser of reward and punishment, so it is hardly surprising that Kant should insist that God demands payment of any outstanding debt of sin.

If punishment cannot be fully exacted *before* conversion and does not seem appropriate *after* conversion, then it must in some way be exacted *during* conversion (6:73). Drawing on Paul's language, Kant notes that the process of moral conversion involves "the putting off of the old man and the putting on of the new." This means that the human being "dies unto sin . . . in order to live unto justice" (6:74). But these are not really two separate things, since one only abandons an evil disposition by adopting a good one. This conversion, Kant says, again following Paul's language, is a kind of sacrifice that brings with it its own suffering. This suffering constitutes the deserved punishment of the "old man"; all of the sufferings and trials that the human being will encounter as a result of his good disposition, though taken on willingly and for the sake of the good, nevertheless are "fitting punishment" for the old man who, Kant notes, is a different human being morally speaking (6:74). In a way, the debt of sin is paid for by another person: the "new man" pays for the "old man." But this other person is only "other" in a *moral* sense; it is still one and the same *physical* person. Adopting the traditional Christian language of atonement, Kant says that the new man—a "Son of God" on account of his pure disposition—acts as a "vicarious substitute" for the old man. The human being who has undergone a moral conversion is, then, his own savior.

Kant's solution is not without difficulties. For example, Kant insists that one cannot generate a surplus through one's good works to pay off the old debt of sin. But isn't that what is really going on here? Kant lets the sufferings that one experiences as a result of a life dedicated to the good count as punishment for the old self, but doesn't the moral law demand that one endure these sufferings? And if these sufferings are obligatory, how can they do the double work of paying off the debt of sin? Moreover, Kant's entire argument rests upon the idea that even if there is one and the same physical person, there are nevertheless two selves, one of which pays the debt of the other. How seriously are we supposed to take this language of the two selves, the "old man" and the "new man"? If these two selves really are different, then why is atonement a problem for the postconversion self? Why can he not simply dissociate himself from the old self's evil and the old self's guilt? Or, if the two selves are not really different, how can the new self ever really feel himself acquitted before divine justice?

Kant makes a curious comment after providing his solution to the third difficulty: "Here, then, is that surplus over the merit from works for which we felt the need earlier, one which is imputed to us by *grace*" (6:75). The terms "works" and "grace" derive from Paul's letters, and in Lutheran theology in particular, they stand in sharp opposition. "Works" refers to what a person does to *earn* his own salvation, whereas "grace" refers to the salvation that God freely gives, without a person having done anything to merit it. For Luther and other Protestant reformers (though this style of theology ultimately traces back to St Augustine), the human being *cannot* do anything on his own to merit salvation, given his sinful and corrupted nature; we, therefore, rely entirely upon God's grace. Everything that Kant has said about how one becomes pleasing to

God stands in direct contrast to this idea, or so it seemed: Kant's doctrine of salvation, in the *Religion*, is entirely "works" based. Yet here Kant claims to have found a place and perhaps even a need for grace in the process of becoming pleasing to God.

But what exactly does Kant mean by "grace"? That Kant's idea of grace is radically different from the traditional Christian one is made abundantly clear in the following passage:

> For what in our earthly life (and perhaps even in all future times and worlds) is always only in mere *becoming* (namely, our being a human being well-pleasing to God) is imputed to us as if we already possessed it here in full. And to this we indeed have no rightful claim (according to the empirical cognition we have of ourselves), so far as we know ourselves (estimate our disposition not directly but only according to our deeds), so that the accuser within us would still be more likely to render a verdict of guilty. It is always therefore only a decree of grace when we are relieved of all responsibility for the sake of this good in which we believe, though fully in accord with eternal justice (because based on a satisfaction that for us consists only in the idea of an improved disposition of which, however, God alone has cognition). (6:75–76)

Grace consists in attributing to us full possession of something (being well-pleasing to God) that is only in a state of becoming. Assuming that we haven't yet achieved this state, having it attributed to us would count as a gift from God. But Kant doesn't actually say here that we are not well-pleasing to God; he says that we have no rightful claim to count ourselves as well-pleasing to God "according to the empirical cognition we have of ourselves." In other words, it is *not* the case that we haven't earned our own salvation; it is simply the case that we cannot *know* that we have earned it because we cannot know our dispositions. We, therefore, invariably judge ourselves to be guilty, so that a "not guilty" verdict can only be experienced as a "decree of grace." Of course, one might ask, is this still really grace? Or is Kant doing something we've seen him do before (with terms like "innate" and "nature" in his discussion of radical evil), using a term in a way that is basically opposite to its ordinary meaning? Whether or not Kant ultimately makes room for grace in the *Religion*—and if so, what exactly this grace consists of—is a question that many scholars have debated, and one that is raised in any careful reading of this text.

Kant, then, has provided an account in this third difficulty of how a person can become well-pleasing to God, even though he has incurred a debt of sin prior to his moral conversion. The problem of how a sinner can be made righteous in God's eyes is, as mentioned earlier, the theological problem of justification. Kant refers to his account of the way in which payment is exacted through the process of conversion as a "deduction of the idea of a *justification* of a human being who is indeed guilty but has passed into a disposition well-pleasing to God." He claims that this deduction is an attempt to answer to a "speculative question," and he asks whether this deduction is of any practical use (6:76). After all, Kant's question, in dealing with these difficulties, has been how a person who has adopted a good disposition can be pleasing to God, despite past evil and a slow and endless road to perfection. But this presupposes that the person already has a good disposition. So, Kant's speculations cannot be helpful in getting a person to adopt a good disposition in the first place.

Kant does say, however, that providing an answer to this "speculative question" is important; for if the question cannot be answered, reason could be accused of being unable to reconcile the human being's hope for forgiveness with divine justice, which would no doubt be morally disadvantageous (6:76). This was precisely the explanation Kant gave for the necessity of engaging in the *parergonal* reflection of the General Remarks; it seems that his *parergonal* exercise in speculative thought has seeped out into the main exposition.

Moreover, Kant notes that his deduction of justification can be put to a *negative* use: while it does not demonstrate precisely how expiation happens, as this is a "speculative question," it does demonstrate that none of the various ways in which historical religions attempt to expiate this debt of sin can substitute for a genuine change of moral disposition (6:76). Therefore, whatever else one makes of Kant's theological speculations, they serve to translate traditional doctrines into ones that are consonant with morality and rebuff the pretensions of any religious practices other than a revolution in disposition to put us in good standing with God.

Section Two: Concerning the evil principle's rightful claim to dominion over the human being, and the struggle of the two principles with one another

Every human being is engaged in a struggle to overcome evil and establish a good disposition. The enemy, as Kant established earlier in Part II, is an "internal" one; yet scripture represents the struggle between good and evil in the form of a story that narrates the struggle between two powers—external to the human being—that vie for control over him. Kant recounts this story, which begins with the Fall of Adam and Eve and ends with the death and resurrection of Jesus. Of course, Kant is still not using the name "Jesus" here, since he is reading scripture as representing the prototype of human moral perfection.

Satan, an originally good being who inexplicably became evil, represents the evil principle. His rebellion against God caused his expulsion from heaven; he then sought to establish his dominion over the minds of Adam and Eve, who had been set up by God as proprietors of the goods of the earth. By causing them to rebel against God, Satan set *himself* up as proprietor of the earth, establishing a "Kingdom of Evil." Adam's descendants were subjugated to this Kingdom of Evil, but freely consented to this subjugation, allowing themselves to be distracted by the goods of this world from the damnation awaiting them (6:79).

Kant notes that despite the dominion of this Kingdom of Evil, the good principle kept hold in the world through a form of government directed to the veneration of the good principle: Jewish theocracy (6:79). It may seem odd that Kant refers to Judaism not as a religion but as a "form of government." As we will see, Kant believes that Christianity is the sole moral religion, and since moral religion is the true religion, any religion that is not ethical fails to be a religion. Recall from our discussion of Kant's ethics in Part I the distinction between morality and legality. One's actions are legal if they agree with the moral law, whatever incentives might have induced those actions, but one only acts morally if one acts out of respect for the moral law. In the simplest terms, incentives for actions make no difference with respect to legality, but they make all the difference with respect to morality. According to Kant, Judaism is a government with God as king and the Jewish people as God's subjects. God gives the Jewish people commands (the 613 laws that God gives to Moses on Mount Sinai, and which form the basis for Jewish religious practice), some of which are ethical ("Thou shalt not kill") and many of which pertain to what we would consider ritual or ceremonial observance. Even though some of these laws are explicitly ethical, Judaism does not qualify as a moral religion, according to Kant, because the Jewish people were not commanded to perform these "ethical" actions out of respect for the moral law but out of fear of punishment and the promise of earthly reward.

Jesus, however, introduced a revolution from within the Jewish religion—a revolution that, Kant remarks, may well have been influenced by Greek moral teachings. Scripture and Christian doctrine represent Jesus as having been born without implication in the sin of the Adam and Eve, and therefore free from Satan's temptations. Since he could exert no influence over Jesus' mind, Satan did the only thing he could do: make Jesus' earthly existence miserable through suffering, persecution, and death. The struggle between good and evil, represented by the persons of Jesus and Satan, is, therefore, a victory for Satan when considered in *physical* terms. But Satan is ultimately unable to rule over Jesus' mind and thus the minds of any who choose to follow him. Although we cannot say that evil has been conquered, its controlling power is loosened through the demonstration of another possible dominion, that of freedom, wherein no one is subject to the dominion of evil unless he willingly submit himself to it (6:82). By succumbing to death for the sake of the good, Jesus becomes a manifestation of this freedom, and therefore of the possibility of human moral perfection and the victory of good over evil.

General Remark

Kant's *parergon* to Part II is about miracles and, to a lesser extent, about the danger that accompanies belief in them. Kant begins this Remark with the declaration that for moral religion to be established on earth, the miracles that are associated with the beginning of this moral religion must be rendered dispensable. Note that Kant does *not* say that people must stop believing in miracles. Rather, in saying that miracles must become *dispensable*, he means that religion *must not depend upon or derive support from* miracles for its validity. Moral religion, for Kant, consists in the disposition to observe one's duties as divine commands (6:84). Failure to grant authority to the moral precepts dictated by reason unless they are first validated and authenticated by miracles constitutes, as we have seen, "moral unbelief."

To understand what Kant is doing in this General Remark, it is helpful to keep in mind where he is ultimately headed: to the claim that Christianity alone among the historical faiths is a moral religion, as the teachings of Christianity's founder are essentially moral teachings (he will make this argument in Part IV). So, when Kant claims here that it is completely conformable to the usual human way of thinking that the historical introduction of a moral religion should be accompanied by miracles to signal the end of the old religion of "mere cult and observances," he is referring to the miracles associated with Jesus and the disciples recorded in scripture, which mark the end of Judaism and the birth of Christianity. But these miracles are not in any way necessary for this new religion, since a moral religion does not *need* miracles to lend it its authority, as a religion of mere cult and observances always does. At the same time, there is no need to contest the claim that there were miracles associated with the birth of this new religion. These miracles are now irrelevant; moral religion stands firm on its own. Specifically, there is no need to contest belief in the miraculous nature of this religion's founder, nor in his miraculous appearance on the earth and departure from it, nor in the miraculous way in which these miracles themselves are made known, namely through supernatural revelation. All of these beliefs may be left untouched, even respected for having served as an "external cover" that helped make public a doctrine "whose authentication rests on a document indelibly retained in every soul and in need of no miracle" (6:85). They may be left untouched, that is, so long as we do not make knowing or professing belief in miracles a condition of becoming well-pleasing to God (ibid.)

Kant's statement that such miracles need not be challenged is a very small concession to Christian orthodoxy, particularly since he has insisted all along that transcendent claims can never really be challenged anyway, as humans are not in a position to know whether any such claims are true or false. There is a tremendous challenge to Christian orthodoxy, however, in the claim that belief in, or profession of, these miracles—which includes nothing less than belief in the incarnation and resurrection of Jesus Christ and in the divine origin of scripture—is entirely inessential for moral religion.

Kant goes on to describe a class of rational believers who are not inclined to renounce belief in miracles, though they never allow this belief to have any practical bearing on how they live their lives. This stance is reflected in the policy of "wise governments" to allow that miracles used to occur in ancient times but to deny that they occur any longer. In this way, they forestall any disturbance to the public order that might come from new miracle workers (6:85–6). Kant does not explain precisely why miracle workers pose a threat to public order, but he no doubt has in mind the fact that the claim to be able to work miracles is implicitly a claim to authority, which can, in turn, be used to challenge existing structures of authority, religious or political.

Kant proceeds to offer a definition of miracles ("events in the world, the causes and *effects* of which are absolutely unknown to us and so must remain") and to divide miracles into two classes, theistic and demonic, with the latter dividing further into satanic and angelic miracles (6:86). Of course, miracles don't come with helpful little identifying labels, so, the obvious question is, how does one distinguish between them? Kant quickly dismisses angelic miracles: good angels, he remarks, "give us little or nothing at all to say about them" (6:86). As for theistic miracles, Kant says that reason has a "negative criterion" it can employ: "if something is represented as commanded by God in a direct manifestation of him yet is directly in conflict with morality, it cannot be a divine miracle despite every appearance of being one" (6:87). Kant's example here is the famous story known as the *akedah* or "binding" of Isaac from Genesis 22. In this story, God commands Abraham to sacrifice his son Isaac. Abraham accedes to God's command and is stopped by an angelic intervention right before bringing down the knife. The miracle that concerns Kant in this story is not the appearance of the angel at the end of the story but the initial voice that Abraham hears commanding him to sacrifice his son: Can this "miracle," one that commands murder, truly have come from God? Kant's answer is a decisive no, because the command itself runs counter to morality. Assuming that this miracle took place, it would have to be a demonic miracle. However, we cannot conclude that a miracle is theistic simply because it accords with morality; as Kant says, "the evil spirit often acts the part, as they say, of an angel of light" (6:87). Thus, we cannot conclude that the voice commanding Abraham to stop the sacrifice was theistic or angelic (indeed it might even have been satanic), but we can conclude that whatever Abraham heard that set him on the path to filicide could not have come from God.

Part III: The victory of the good principle over the evil principle, and the founding of a kingdom of God on earth

The human being must himself carry out the revolution in disposition required to become well-pleasing to God; no one else can do the work for him. Indeed, the radical evil that Kant describes in Part I, as well as the struggle against this evil described in Part II, is presented as a more or less *individual* affair. In Part III, the social dimension of the struggle against evil comes to the forefront. In the opening paragraphs of Part III, Kant says that the prize one wins through the successful struggle against evil is simply freedom from the *dominion* of evil; one is not freed, however, from the perpetual *onslaught* of evil, and one must stay perpetually armed for battle (6:93).

Kant then proceeds to make the pregnant suggestion that if one searches for the causes that keep one in this state of constant danger, one can be easily convinced that they come not from one's "own raw nature," so far as one exists in isolation, but rather from others with whom one associates. As a solitary being, the human has few needs and a rather tranquil frame of mind. His passions are aroused, however, as soon as he is among other humans beings: "He is poor (or considers himself so) only to the extent that he is anxious that other human beings will consider him poor and will despise him for it. Envy, addiction to power, avarice, and the malignant inclinations associated with these, assail his nature, which on its own is undemanding, *as soon as he is among human beings.*" It is not even necessary that these humans with whom he associates be evil themselves; so long as there are other humans around, they *will* corrupt each other (6:93–94).

This claim calls to mind Kant's analysis in Part I of the "predisposition to humanity" (6:26–27). This predisposition, you will recall, is a form of self-love that consists in the almost mechanical tendency to compare oneself with others and to judge oneself happy only by comparison with them. This desire to gain worth in the eyes of others quickly becomes the desire to acquire superiority over others, yielding what Kant calls the "vices of culture," which include envy, ingratitude, and joy in others' misfortunes (6:27). Described in these terms, this predisposition to humanity hardly sounds like a "predisposition to good in human nature." But Kant considers it to be a predisposition to the good because this inborn competitiveness is a means that nature employs as "an incentive to culture," and this predisposition does not in itself preclude "reciprocal love." Nevertheless, this predisposition to humanity is double-edged, and in this respect, it parallels the predisposition to animality; both predispositions are natural or mechanical forms of self-love that bring benefit to humans, provided they are subordinated to the moral law. When these forms of self-love are allowed free reign, however, they bring vice in their wake. But the resulting vice is not itself natural, even if it is made possible by these natural forms of self-love, for vice only results from the free choice to subordinate the moral law to self-love.

Kant's suggestion in Part III that human association may be largely responsible for moral corruption has led some scholars such as Allen Wood to conclude that "the radical evil in human nature arises and manifests itself only in the social condition" (Wood 2010b, 261). In other words, despite the predominantly individualist emphasis in Part I, such scholars would argue that the human propensity to evil is essentially social and therefore only given full expression here in Part III. Another name for this radical evil in human nature, Wood claims, is "unsocial sociability," a phrase found not in the *Religion* but in the Fourth Proposition of the "Idea for a Universal History with a Cosmopolitan Aim" (1784):

> *The means which nature employs to bring about the development of innate capacities is that of antagonism within society, in so far as this antagonism becomes in the long run the cause of a law-governed social order.* By antagonism, I mean in this context

the *unsocial sociability* of men, that is, their tendency to come together in society, coupled, however, with a continual resistance which constantly threatens to break this society up. (44)

Is society ultimately the key to understanding what Kant means by radical evil? Whatever answer one gives to this question, it is perfectly clear that for Kant, overcoming evil requires that action be taken on the social, and not merely on the individual, level. Unless humans establish a union aimed at the prevention of this mutual corruption, they are in constant danger of relapse into evil. It is, therefore, a duty of the entire human race to establish such a society (6:94). It will be the task of Division One to delineate the features of this society and to articulate the role that historical religion can and should play in its formation.

Division One: Philosophical representation of the victory of the good principle in the founding of a kingdom of God on earth

I Concerning the ethical state of nature (6:95–96)

Humans have a duty to establish a society to combat the evil that arises through mutual corruption; Kant calls this society an "ethical community," which he contrasts with a "juridico-civil" or *political* state. Much of Kant's argument in Division One turns upon this distinction. A political state, according to Kant, is one in which human beings stand under public juridical laws. These laws are *coercive*, which is to say that the sovereign has the power to enforce compliance with them. These juridical laws are, of course, enforceable because the sovereign is only concerned that the actions of its citizens *conform* to the laws; for example, the sovereign wants its citizens to obey the law not to steal but is presumably indifferent to the underlying reasons for compliance with this law. Or perhaps it is better to say that the sovereign has no choice but to be indifferent to the underlying motives for compliance with the law, because the sovereign is not able to perceive the underlying dispositions from which actions are taken. As such, it should really make no difference to the sovereign whether one refrains from stealing out of fear of punishment, out of a sense of moral duty, or from the feelings of embarrassment and shame that would result from being caught. The important point is that one follows the law. To put it in Kantian terms, the political state functions on the basis of legality (acting in conformity with the law) rather than morality (acting out of respect for the moral law).

One can see from this account of the political state that such a state can exist in the absence of truly moral actions, even if it cannot exist in the absence of legal actions. As such, a political community is not sufficient to combat moral evil; an ethical community is required. An ethical community is a community of people united under *moral* laws. Unlike the juridical laws of the political state, these moral laws are not coercive. The sovereign, as we know, is in no position to enforce morality because the sovereign cannot see the moral dispositions underlying action; but there is another reason why moral laws cannot be coercive. An action only has moral worth if it results from the person's free power of choice. Moral action, therefore, cannot be coerced, because external coercion stands in opposition to freedom. Therefore, whereas humans can be coerced to move from a political state of nature into a political state, humans cannot be coerced to move from an ethical state of nature into an ethical community. They must freely choose to do so. This means that people can be a part of an existing political state and yet at the same time be in an ethical state of nature.

Finally, Kant says that the concept of an ethical community is an ideal that includes the union of *all* human beings; in this way, too, it is distinct from a political state, which includes only a smaller subset of the human population. Therefore, a group of people within one particular society united under ethical principles does not yet constitute an ethical community; this group of people must strive to establish an ethical whole that embraces all of humanity. Only then will this ideal of an ethical community be attained.

II The human being ought to leave the ethical state of nature in order to become a member of an ethical community (6:96–98)

Just as humans have a duty to leave behind the state of nature and enter into a political state, so too do humans have a duty to leave behind the ethical state of nature—a state in which they corrupt one another's moral dispositions—and enter into an ethical community. In both political and ethical states of nature, the human being is the author of his own laws, acknowledges no external laws, and is subject to no external authority. Leaving the political state of nature requires acceptance of an external authority (a sovereign) to administer and enforce laws. But what is required to leave an ethical state of nature? Kant will address this further on. Here, he simply points out that we have a duty to leave the ethical state of nature, and moreover, that this duty is of a unique sort: it is not a duty that individual humans have toward other humans, but rather a duty that the human race as a whole has toward itself. But what exactly does it mean to say that the species as a whole has a duty? Kant's reasoning here is as follows: Every species of rational being has a common end: the promotion of the highest good, which is a good common to all. This end can only be brought about through the cooperation of all people united in a common purpose; it is not within the power of any isolated individual to achieve it. Therefore, the duty to bring about an ethical community is unlike other moral duties, which require us to do only what is within our own power. This duty is a collective duty of the species, since only the species as a whole can bring it about (6:97–98).

But can the human race as a whole really bring about an ethical community? If it is not possible, then it cannot be a duty. Kant actually makes a curious remark that suggests that it may not, in fact, be possible for the human race to accomplish this goal by its own power: "We can already anticipate that this duty will need the presupposition of another idea, namely, of a higher moral being through whose universal organization the forces of single individuals, insufficient on their own, are united for a common effect" (6:98). He says more about the role of this higher being in the following section.

III The concept of an ethical community is the concept of a people of God under ethical laws (6:98–100)

Like a political community, an ethical community requires public laws—issued by a common lawgiver—to which all members are bound. Since legislation in a political state is coercive and not moral, there is no particular problem regarding the people themselves as the author of these juridico-civil laws. The legislation in a political state derives, Kant says, from the principle of *"limiting the freedom of each to the conditions under which it can coexist with the freedom of everyone else, in accordance with a universal law"* (6:98). The details of this principle—which form the subject of the "Doctrine of Right," the first part of Kant's *Metaphysics of Morals*—need not detain us here; the important point is that since juridico-civil legislation consists in limiting the individual's use of freedom so as to enable it to coexist with the freedom of others, this legislation does not require any insight into the morality of the actions of the members of the state.

By contrast, the people themselves cannot be regarded as the sovereign lawgiver in an ethical community, since the morality of an action is not visible to the human eye. The ethical community requires a sovereign who can see the very dispositions underlying actions and dispense justice in accordance with moral worth, not mere legality. This is not to say, however, that the laws derive from the will of this lawgiver and are, therefore, arbitrarily imposed upon the citizens of this ethical community. For Kant, moral laws are laws that rational beings give to themselves (this is the meaning of *autonomy*); any laws externally imposed upon a rational being—whether these laws derive from the will of another being, including God, or even from the laws of nature—are *heteronomous* and therefore not moral. So, it cannot be that the sovereign of the ethical community simply imposes his laws upon its citizens; rather, these moral laws must be simultaneously the will of this supreme lawgiver. (In Part IV, as we will see, Kant defines religion precisely as the recognition of one's moral duties as divine commands.) This supreme lawgiver whose commands are at the same time moral laws, and who is capable of seeing the disposition, determining one's moral worth, and dispensing happiness in proportion to it, is none other than God. Thus, Kant concludes, an ethical community is a community of people united under divine commands in accordance with moral laws.

It is also possible to think of a people united under God in accordance with statutory laws—that is, laws that derive merely from the will of the lawgiver and are, therefore, not moral laws. This form of government would be called a "theocracy." Despite the fact that God is the sovereign of this state, it does not differ in essence from a political state; such a community of people, therefore, does not qualify as an ethical community. Kant will understand Judaism in precisely this way, though that discussion will have to wait until Division Two.

IV The idea of a people of God cannot be realized (by human organization) except in the form of a church (6:100–102)

Kant opens this section with a healthy dose of skepticism concerning the ability of human beings to actually establish such an ethical community on their own; this ideal, he says, is "greatly scaled down under human hands." The conditions of sensuous human nature place limitations on the ability of humans to achieve this end. Echoing once more the *Idea for a Universal History with a Cosmopolitan Aim*, Kant asks how one could "expect to construct something completely straight from such crooked wood"; whereas this question in the *Idea for a Universal History* was posed with respect to the political state, here it is posed with respect to the ethical community.

Founding a moral people of God, Kant says, is something that only God can do, not humans. But humans cannot sit around waiting for God to act. Indeed, there is a parallel here to Kant's discussion of grace in Part II; just as divine assistance can only reasonably be hoped for when one has done everything in one's power to make oneself a better person, so too can divine assistance on a social level only reasonably be hoped for when society has done everything in its power to bring about an ethical community. Only if each person acts "as if everything depended on him" can he hope that God will make up the difference (6:101). What is it, then, that humans *can* do?

Kant does not answer this question straightaway; instead, he introduces the concept of the "church," and distinguishes between the "church invisible" and the "church visible." First of all, Kant makes it clear that by church, he means nothing other than the ethical community under divine legislation, the very thing he discussed in the previous section; so "church" is not a new concept after all. By the church invisible, Kant refers to the idea of the community of all morally "upright" human beings united under the divine sovereign.

Because we can never know whether, in fact, a particular community consists of all morally upright beings—since we cannot perceive the disposition—this church is "invisible." The church invisible is an idea of reason, and since this idea of reason is something that humans are to emulate in their construction of an ethical community, the church invisible is a prototype. (Here, the translation says "archetype" rather than "prototype," but the German word is the very same one that we encountered in Part II in connection with "Jesus" as the prototype of moral perfection: *Urbild*. What the Son of God is for the individual, the church invisible is for humans collectively.)

The church visible, by contrast, is the actual human community modeled upon this prototype, though it invariably falls short of the prototype. What is a visible church like? First of all, since every community under public laws requires subordination of some of its members to others, who are charged with teaching and overseeing the observance of these laws, the church visible will be divided into a "congregation" and "servants of the church"; while these servants of the church occupy a higher position than the rest of the congregation, they are nevertheless called "servants" because they themselves only tend to the affairs of the "invisible head" of the church, God (6:101).

Kant goes on to say that a "true" visible church is one that approximates the church invisible as closely as possible and therefore possesses the following marks: (1) It will be *universal*, since a true church is *moral*, and morality is universal; a true visible church, therefore, can never be divided against itself in its essential purpose, even if there are accidental (nonessential) differences within the church. (2) The church will be *pure*, which is to say that the union of its members will be based upon nothing other than moral incentives, and will, therefore, be free of superstition and enthusiasm. (3) The relation between members of the church will be one of *freedom*; since the church is a moral community, there must be no compulsion to membership. Moreover, this relation of freedom must extend to the relationship between church and state. (4) Finally, the constitution of the church is *unchangeable*; while there may be some accidental regulations for the administration of the church that change over time, the basic principles of the church, since they are moral principles, will not change.

Finally, Kant notes that because the visible church is a representative of a state ruled by God, it has nothing in common with the political constitution of the state and therefore is not monarchic, aristocratic, or democratic. Instead, Kant likens the church to a family, united under an invisible moral father (God). The son—that is, the prototype of moral perfection from Part II—"knows the father's will" and makes the rest of the family "better acquainted with his will." The family, therefore, honors the father in the son, and the whole family becomes a "free, universal, and enduring union of hearts" (6:102). The Christological language here is certainly a clue that Kant is thinking of the Christian church as *a*, if not *the*, "true visible church."

V The constitution of each and every church always proceeds from some historical (revealed) faith, which we can call ecclesiastical faith; and this is best founded on a holy scripture (6:102–109)

If universality is a mark of the true church, then it stands to reason that such a church must be founded upon a purely *rational* (moral) faith. Since morality is universal, a religion based upon morality will be universal as well. And yet, on account of a certain "weakness of human nature," this pure faith alone can never entirely be relied upon to found a church (6:103). In this section, Kant argues that humans are not easily convinced that what God requires of them is a morally good life; instead, they inevitably seek to find other, nonmoral ways to serve God, replacing moral religion with a religion of divine service. Kant claims that since every "great lord" on earth wishes to be honored and praised by his subjects by signs of submissiveness, humans reason that God must wish to be honored in this way as well. Kant will have much more to say about this in Part IV; there he attributes the tendency of humans to a religion of divine service to the desire to avoid the strenuous moral labor of becoming better people, such that they form an anthropomorphic concept of God built precisely on the model of a human ruler.

But what is wrong with thinking that God wishes to be honored just as humans wish to be honored? After all, there is certainly plenty of scriptural language that suggests that God does wish to be honored. Kant signals that there is something misguided about this way of thinking. He says that it never occurs to many people that through moral action, humans are constantly serving God and that God cannot, in fact, be served in any other way, since humans are not capable of exerting any influence upon God (6:103). Why isn't it possible for humans to exercise their influence on God? Kant doesn't say, but there are a number of possibilities. Perhaps Kant is thinking here in traditional theological terms, in which God is often said to be *impassible*, incapable of being emotionally affected by another being; this would no doubt include feeling the effects of flattery. Or perhaps Kant is thinking that God, as an intelligible being that transcends nature, is not subject to causal laws and therefore is incapable of being influenced by other beings. Or perhaps Kant is simply thinking that insofar as the idea of God he is working with is the idea of God generated by practical reason, this God is, by definition, only interested in the moral behavior of his creatures. Whatever Kant has in mind here, the point is clear: a rational religion is a religion in which moral action alone is pleasing to God; any attempt to serve God in another way is fundamentally misguided. In Part IV, Kant will diagnose the attempt to influence a supernatural being (God) through natural means (nonmoral human actions) as "fetishism."

Kant, thus, distinguishes between two ways of thinking about God's legislative will: (1) as commanding through merely statutory laws and (2) as commanding through moral laws (6:104). In the latter case, each person is capable of discerning the will of God through his own reason; in fact, the idea of God actually derives from his consciousness of his moral responsibility, as well as from his need to postulate the existence of a higher being in order to bring about the highest good in this world. This gives rise to the idea of a single purely moral religion. (This, in a nutshell, is the idea of God and religion that Kant developed in his previous writings, and that he spells out, albeit rather tersely, in the Preface to the first edition of the *Religion*.) However, if God's commands were not moral but statutory, then we could not know them through our own reason; instead, we would have to know them through some historical revelation. Statutory legislation, then, presents us with an important problem: if this legislation cannot be known through reason but is only made known historically, then there will be plenty of human beings who have never received this revelation. No statutory legislation can be valid for every human being, and therefore, a universal church must be founded upon a religion that conceives of God as legislating through *moral* laws. Referring to Matthew 7.21,

Kant says that "'not they who say Lord! Lord! But they who do the will of God,'"—that is, those who seek to please God through good life conduct—will be the ones who worship God properly.

Let's step back for a moment and take stock of the argument thus far. Kant first distinguished between a political state and an ethical community, arguing that the human race has a duty to itself to establish the ethical community. Next, he argued that this ethical community must be conceived of as a people of God united under moral laws, which he calls a "church." He then made a distinction between the invisible and visible church. The invisible church represents the ideal ethical community, a prototype to be emulated by the visible church. Finally, Kant argued that the true visible church must be founded upon public laws that are universal, and that the only laws that will work here are *moral* laws, since statutory laws are historically contingent and cannot be universalized.

Now, if delineating the features of the true church is, for Kant, rather straightforward, the implementation of the true church is a decidedly messy affair. In the church invisible, the only legislation is moral legislation and all humans are united in their "upright" moral dispositions. But in a visible church—not an ideal one, but an actual historical institution—not everyone is united in moral disposition; indeed, the whole point of the visible church is to work toward this ideal union. Therefore, moral laws will not be sufficient; the church visible requires a "*public* form of obligation, some ecclesiastical form that depends on experiential conditions and is intrinsically contingent and manifold" (6:105). When Kant speaks of the "public form of obligation," he is referring to the particular, contingent statutes and forms of worship that unite a particular ecclesiastical body, that is, the rituals, liturgy, scripture, and dogmas of a particular ecclesiastical faith. These public forms of obligation are certainly not universal, since they do not derive from reason; they are, therefore, statutory. Nevertheless, as we will see, these statutory laws can be put into the service of moral religion as the vehicle or means for its promotion.

As always, Kant insists that we cannot wait around for God to hand us an ecclesiastical faith to serve as a vehicle, nor should we facilely conclude that the statutes of some particular ecclesiastical faith are, in fact, divine. Of course, we have no way of verifying that such statutes are divine anyway; but Kant's point here is that if we declare these statutes divine, then we are wrongly alleviating ourselves of the burden to improve the form of the church so that it better approximates the church invisible. Nevertheless, having recognized that ecclesiastical faith is required to serve as the vehicle for the promotion of a pure religious faith, Kant says that it would be "arrogant" to deny out of hand that a particular ecclesiastical faith might, in fact, be a "special divine dispensation" if it turns out that the church's teachings are in harmony with moral religion. Kant will argue in Part IV that Christianity is just such an ecclesiastical faith.

We need not invent anew the statutes and public forms of worship that the invisible church requires for the development of an ethical community. Philosophically speaking, pure religious faith has priority, since the visible church is to be modeled upon the invisible church, just as the particular imperfect human being is to model himself upon the prototype of moral perfection. But in point of fact, particular ecclesiastical communities, aiming at divine service through the fulfillment of statutory commands, always *precede* pure religious faith; as Kant says, temples always come before churches, and priests always come before ministers (6:106). Statutory faith is always already there. This is so simply because of the human propensity to believe that God wishes to be served not through a moral life but through compliance with arbitrary precepts and commands. Kant concludes, then, that ecclesiastical faith (i.e., a historical faith based upon revealed, statutory laws) is not *added to* pure religious faith as a vehicle for its transmission; rather, ecclesiastical faith always comes first and the true church proceeds from it, as Kant says succinctly in the title of this section.

Finally, Kant claims that religious faith is best diffused not through mere traditions but through scripture. Even those who cannot read the holy books revere them and their interpreters, and faiths based upon tradition and public observances disappear once the state falls (like the cults of ancient Rome and Greece). Thus, given the superiority of scripture to traditions, Kant says how "fortunate" it is that a book should have "fallen into human hands" that contains not only the statutes necessary for a visible church, but also a pure moral doctrine that can be "brought into the strictest harmony" with those statutes. Such a book, Kant says, is capable of commanding an authority on a par with that of revelation (6:107). The book Kant has in mind, of course, is the Bible, or more specifically, the New Testament. (As we will see in Part IV, Kant has serious doubts about the value of the Old Testament.)

Kant concludes this section with a few terminological notes, the most important of which is his distinction between *religion* and *faith*. The word "religion," Kant insists, should be reserved only for true moral religion; the merely historical so-called religions (Judaism, Islam, Christianity, etc.) should be called *faiths*. Because there is only one true moral religion, any differences between believers will always be differences in faith, not differences in religion. The various "religious struggles" that have resulted in so much bloodshed are nothing other than struggles between particular ecclesiastical faiths. Indeed, one can only be prevented by an intolerant state from practicing one's faith; a state can never prevent the practice of true religion, which as we know, consists in nothing other than moral conduct (6:107–108).

VI Ecclesiastical faith has the pure faith of religion for its supreme interpreter (6:109–114)

Religion (by which Kant means true moral religion, as we have just seen) is caught in a double bind. On the one hand, as soon as it is tied to a historical faith, it loses its universality. And yet, it cannot do without any historical faith, "because of the natural need of all human beings to demand for even the highest concepts and grounds of reason something that *the senses can hold on to*, some confirmation from experience or the like" (6:109). Historical faith, then, is needed as a vehicle for true moral religion, even though it compromises the universality of true moral religion. So, the question is: how can a particular, historical faith be united with a universal moral faith?

The answer is *interpretation*. We begin with whatever supposed revelation we have at hand and interpret it so that it harmonizes with the universal moral laws of pure religion. But what happens if the plain meaning of the text does not harmonize with the principles of moral religion? Kant's response is perhaps surprising: he does not hesitate to claim that such a moral interpretation should be "forced" onto the text "if the text can at all bear it," and that this forced interpretation is more desirable than a literal interpretation which does not promote, or even runs counter to, morality (6:110). Through interpretation, we can take a supposed revelation from a particular historical faith and make its contents appear identical to the principles of moral religion. Interpretation enables us to utilize the historical as a vehicle for the universal.

In the following paragraph, Kant tries to allay any concerns about "forcing" a moral interpretation onto a particular revelation by pointing out that many different faiths—including Christianity—interpret their scriptures in just such a fashion. (As we will see in a moment, the responsibility of *getting scripture right*, as it were, falls not to the moral interpreter, but to the *scriptural scholar*.) Be that as it may, the ubiquity of such practice is hardly a very solid defense. But Kant adds to this the claim that revelation can often be given a moral interpretation without a too flagrant violation of its literal meaning because of the predisposition to moral religion hidden in human reason; while it may have been the practice of divine service that initially gave rise to these supposed revelations, the predisposition to moral religion made itself heard and wove itself into these "poetic fabrications" (6:111). However compelling these claims might be, they are ultimately irrelevant in light of what follows. For in the very next line, Kant says that such moral interpretations cannot be accused of dishonesty, as long as one does not claim that these interpretations represent the true intentions of the authors of these texts; the moral interpreter only claims that it is *possible* that this is what the authors intended. The moral interpreter does not aim to recover the true intention of the author; he represents only one kind of interpreter engaged in one kind of interpretation. Alongside him stands a very different kind of interpreter, the scriptural scholar.

The scriptural scholar, according to Kant, has two aims: the *certification* of scripture and the *exposition* of scripture (6:113). What does Kant mean by "certification"? Assuming that an ecclesiastical faith cannot, due to human limitations, dispense altogether with revelation (as a purely moral religion would), the authority of this revelation must be "historically authenticated" through an investigation into its origins. While one cannot "climb up into heaven" to ascertain the authority of this revelation, the scriptural scholar can at least investigate whether there is anything in its origin that would make its acceptance as divine revelation impossible. Kant does not provide an example here, but perhaps he is thinking something like this: If a particular scripture claims to be a divine revelation given through a prophet 2000 years ago, and yet an investigation into the language and history of that time makes it unlikely that this alleged revelation is, in fact, 2000 years old, then there may be good reason to doubt that this text is, in fact, divine revelation. Thus, while scriptural scholarship cannot show that a particular scripture *is* divine revelation, it can at least establish that it is not impossible for it to be so. As for the "exposition" of scripture, Kant points out that the scriptural scholar must possess a knowledge of the original languages of scripture as well as a knowledge of historical context (including customs and popular religious beliefs) in order to understand what these texts meant to the communities for which they were written. It is the scriptural scholar, then, not the moral interpreter, who is primarily concerned with understanding the authorial intent of a given text; he brings his linguistic and historical knowledge to bear in discerning this meaning.

Kant goes on to reject the claims of a third interpreter of scripture, one who utilizes neither reason nor scholarship to interpret the meaning of a text and ascertain its divine origin, but instead makes use of "inner feeling" (6:113). Kant, of course, is ever suspicious of the claims of "feeling," precisely because feeling is a private matter and provides no publicly utilizable criteria for determining the genuineness of revelation. By contrast, the religion of reason is properly universal. Therefore, the possible divine origin of a revelation can be ascertained through the universally discernible criterion of the compatibility of this revelation with rational religion. And while scriptural scholarship ultimately becomes "just a faith in scholars and in their insight" (6:114), the claims of these scholars are nevertheless open to scrutiny and can be assessed on the basis of evidence. Therefore, religion of reason and scholarship stand alone as the two rightful expositors of scripture. Only the religion of reason is universally valid, however, since merely historical arguments by definition can never be universally convincing (a point to which Kant will return in his discussion of "learned religion" in Part IV).

We should take note, finally, of Kant's insistence that neither the religion of reason nor scriptural scholarship should be hindered in making "public use" of their insights by the secular authorities. It is important to note that when Kant says "public," he means what we would call "private" (as readers of Kant's "What is Enlightenment?" are aware). In other words, Kant is not advocating for the right of these interpreters to use the pulpit as a forum in which to express these ideas; he is advocating, however, for the freedom of philosophers and biblical scholars to engage in discourse directed toward other philosophers and scholars, free from being censored by the government or bound by confessions of faith in certain religious dogmas. As we have seen, Kant was personally affected by such censorship on account of the publication of the *Religion*, and his defense consisted, in part, in the claim that his book was unintelligible to the public and only intended for debate among scholars (see the chapter on "Context").

VII The gradual transition of ecclesiastical faith toward the exclusive dominion of pure religious faith is the coming of the kingdom of God (6:115–124)

This final section of Division One is certainly the most challenging, but also the most interesting, since it is here that Kant directly grapples with the tension between ecclesiastical (historical) faith and moral faith. Kant begins by reminding us that the distinguishing mark of the true church is universality. Since a historical faith is only valid for those who are in contact with the history upon which it rests, its validity is contingent; historical faith, therefore, lacks the universality of the true church. Yet, if this historical faith has within it a principle for continually coming closer to a pure religious faith until the historical faith (as a vehicle of moral faith) can be dispensed with altogether, and if there is a *conscious awareness* that this historical faith is a vehicle for moral faith, then we can consider this historical church as the true one. Conscious awareness of the status of this historical faith as a mere vehicle, as we will see, is crucial; when historical statutes are taken as ends in themselves, they actively undermine rather than promote moral faith.

Kant then introduces a distinction between "saving faith" and "slavish" or "mercenary" faith. "Saving faith," Kant says, is the "faith of every individual receptive to (worthy of) eternal happiness" (6:115); this faith is *one* faith, yet it can be found in various historical faiths, so long as those faiths tend toward the goal of pure religious faith. By contrast, "slavish faith" is the faith of a religion of statutory service, that is, a service that seeks to please God through morally worthless actions; it cannot be considered a saving faith because it is not moral.

In a saving faith, the "hope of blessedness" depends upon two conditions: first, the undoing of past wrongful actions before a moral judge (God); second, the conversion to a new life of moral conduct. Accordingly, this saving faith requires (1) faith in the satisfaction of one's past sins (in other words, the removal of moral guilt and the payment of the debt of sin), which the human being cannot bring about on his own; and (2) faith in the ability to engage in future moral conduct and become pleasing to God, which the human being can and should bring about on his own. These two conditions, Kant says, add up to one saving faith. But how exactly are they to be combined? Does faith in the undoing of past wrongs (faith in satisfaction) result in good life conduct? Or does good life conduct produce faith in satisfaction?

It is worth pausing for a moment to take stock of this question. After all, didn't Kant already establish in Part II that any satisfaction for past sins must depend upon a moral conversion? So, why is he raising the question anew here in Part III? Isn't the matter already settled? In a sense, the matter is settled: as we will see, Kant ultimately decides again that moral conduct must precede faith in satisfaction. But the larger question Kant wants to answer in this section demands that the issue be reconsidered. Kant has established that ecclesiastical faith is to be used as a vehicle for the transmission of pure rational faith. But this raises the question of whether pure moral faith can eventually do without ecclesiastical (historical) faith or whether ecclesiastical faith "must always supervene as an essential portion of saving faith over and above the pure religious one" (6:116). Up until this point, Kant has seemed quite sure that the vehicle will eventually pass away once the destination is reached; here, however, he does not sound so confident. He claims that there is a "remarkable antinomy" of human reason that, if left unresolved, will prevent us from answering the question of the long-term necessity of ecclesiastical faith.

An antinomy—a word familiar to readers of Kant's first and second *Critiques*—is a contradiction or conflict between two otherwise reasonable positions. First, Kant will show that it is implausible that faith in satisfaction will elicit good life conduct; then, he will show that it is equally implausible that one can begin with good life conduct without faith in satisfaction. Let's look at both sides of the antinomy in more detail, before addressing Kant's proposed solution to it.

First, Kant establishes the implausibility of believing that a faith in satisfaction could elicit good life conduct; indeed, his contempt for this idea is abundantly clear. If an ecclesiastical faith were to bring news to a sinner that satisfaction for his sins had been made for him, and that to appropriate this satisfaction, he had only to *believe* this news—who could possibly resist? And yet, Kant says, it is inconceivable that a rational being who knows himself to be guilty and deserving of punishment could regard his guilt as being done away with so easily, indeed to the extent that he is now able to embark on the life of moral conduct that eluded him before. Rather, he would have to regard such satisfaction as depending upon him first doing everything within his power to improve himself morally. Therefore, it seems, pure moral faith—which insists on the primacy of moral conduct—would have to take precedence over ecclesiastical faith, with its news of satisfaction.

However, if the human is indeed "corrupt by nature," how can he possibly undergo such a moral conversion? Aware of his transgressions and the power of the evil principle over him, how can he believe in his own capacity for good-life conduct? The only way for him to become capable of a moral life is if he believes himself to be reconciled with God—his past sins paid for and moral guilt removed—and through this faith to be born anew. In this case, faith in a merit that is not his own would have to precede his striving for good life conduct, and ecclesiastical faith would have to take precedence over pure moral faith.

Something about this antinomy, however, seems a bit disingenuous. If Part I of the *Religion* has shown anything, it is that humans must have the ability to undergo a moral conversion to the good. In fact, we saw that Kant redefines the word "nature" in Part I to mean the exact opposite of nature in its ordinary sense. So when Kant asks, beginning his discussion of the second half of the antinomy, how a human "corrupt by nature" can possibly undergo a moral conversion, one might respond to Kant: "According to your own account of what it means to be 'corrupt by nature,' such a moral conversion is certainly possible." One is tempted to conclude, then, that there isn't really any antinomy here at all. Perhaps the question is not so important anyway, since Kant does insist in the end that moral faith must take precedence over ecclesiastical faith and that ecclesiastical faith is ultimately dispensable. But Kant settles this matter on practical, not theoretical, grounds. Theoretically, he insists, the issue cannot be decided. Recall from our discussion of Part I that there is something mysterious about freedom for Kant. We cannot have any insight into the determining cause of a particular free action as we might ask what caused some event in the natural world, because if there were a determining cause for that free act, it would no longer be free. So, the reason that one person freely subordinates self-love to the moral law, while another subordinates the moral law to self-love, is inexplicable, at least as far as human theoretical insight goes. This is why, after laying out the two sides of this antinomy, Kant says that these two positions cannot be reconciled through insight into the causal determination of a human's freedom (what makes a human being become good or bad): answering such a question surpasses the speculative capacity of human reason (6:117–118). If we are going to decide whether faith in satisfaction necessarily precedes the first use of our freedom for good life conduct, we must decide on practical, not theoretical, grounds.

On practical grounds, then, Kant sides with good life conduct over faith in satisfaction. In laying out the first side of the antinomy, Kant has already pointed out the inconceivability of a human being knowing he deserves punishment and yet actually believing that satisfaction can be accomplished without him doing anything of any moral value, and further, the implausibility of faith in foreign satisfaction eliciting moral conduct where it was previously absent. But he adds that good life conduct must come first on practical grounds because, since the moral law commands unconditionally, it must be made the supreme condition of any saving faith. Moreover, since ecclesiastical faith is, as Kant has repeatedly insisted, simply a means for the promotion of pure moral faith, whatever in this ecclesiastical faith concerns theoretical knowledge rather than practical action must only consolidate and complete that maxim of action, not precede it (6:118). Finally, Kant notes that if faith in foreign satisfaction precedes moral action, then faith becomes a duty, and moral action the result of grace. This, of course, is precisely the reverse of what Kant argued for in Part II: good life conduct constitutes unconditional duty, while satisfaction for one's sins is a matter of grace.

Kant might well have ended this section here—but he didn't. His solution to the antinomy merely "cuts the knot" by means of a practical maxim, rather than "disentangling" it theoretically; and while this practical resolution is allowed when dealing with religious issues (since religion is about moral conduct anyway), Kant feels the need to add some remarks in order to satisfy the desire for a theoretical resolution (6:119). But he has told us that this antinomy cannot be resolved by theoretical insight into the use of freedom. So, whatever he is about to propose must take a different tack.

To understand Kant's theoretical solution, we need to keep two points in mind from Part II. First, Kant interprets Jesus in the Christian scriptures as a representation of the ideal of human moral perfection formed by our reason—and because this ideal is a model to be emulated, it is a prototype. Second, he interprets faith in the Son of God (as the moral prototype of human perfection) as faith in one's own ability to live up to this moral ideal, or in other words, faith in our ability to become well-pleasing to God through a good moral disposition. With this in mind, let's consider Kant's solution.

Kant notes that faith in the Son of God—morally interpreted as in Part II—itself refers to a moral idea of reason. It makes no difference, therefore, whether I begin with faith in the Son of God or with pure moral faith (good life conduct); it all comes to the same thing anyway. Yet faith that this prototype *has actually appeared in the world* (in the person of the historical Jesus) is a very different matter. Moral faith must be totally rational, but this is a historical, not a rational, proposition. In this respect, faith in the Son of God is at odds with pure moral faith.

Kant thinks he can resolve this contradiction by pointing out the following. According to this historical faith, this prototype is represented as having come down from heaven to earth, whereas according to moral faith, this prototype is represented as already situated within us. But there is really no contradiction here: in the historical appearance of the Son of God—or as Kant calls him, the "God-man"—it is not what is perceived through the *senses* and cognized by *experience* that constitutes the "true object" of saving faith, but rather what we judge in this God-man as conforming to the prototype that already lies in our own reason. In other words, the only way for us to judge that this God-man is, in fact, the prototype sent down from heaven is if we already have knowledge of this prototype within our own reason as the standard and mark by which to recognize him. So, whether we believe the prototype to have descended from heaven or simply to be present in our own reason, it is still one and the same prototype. The antinomy, Kant concludes, is merely apparent, since it results from regarding "the very same idea, only taken in different relations, as different principles" (6:119).

This solution is not satisfying, though it might not be easy, initially, to see why. Kant's resolution to this antinomy hinges on the claim that the true object of saving faith in the God-man is not what falls to the senses, but rather what our reason recognizes in the God-man as conforming to the prototype already present within our own reason. But ecclesiastical (historical) faith would certainly not concede this point, since ecclesiastical faith insists that it is precisely faith in the historical proposition that has priority. If one dissolves the historical proposition into a rational idea, then the antinomy can be resolved; but the antinomy was generated in the first place by a contradiction between the historical (assigning priority to faith in foreign satisfaction) and the rational (assigning priority to moral conduct). Kant acknowledges as much when he adds that if indeed we wish to make "historical faith in the actuality of an appearance" the condition for saving faith, then we indeed do have a true conflict of maxims concerning which of the two conditions of saving faith one must start from, generated by two entirely different principles—one rational, the other empirical. So, this proposed solution is, in fact, no solution at all, and the conflict between historical and rational faith remains resolvable only on practical grounds.

What lesson can we take away from all of this? The central question of this section is whether humanity can ever entirely dispense with the vehicle of ecclesiastical faith. If one believes faith in the historical claim that foreign satisfaction of one's sin has taken place *must precede good life conduct*, then the answer is no; ecclesiastical faith is not dispensable. However, if one believes that faith in satisfaction of one's sins must follow upon doing everything within one's power to live a moral life, then ecclesiastical faith is dispensable. After all, Kant believes that reason is perfectly capable of generating without any help from ecclesiastical faiths the rational hope that so long as we do everything in our power to be what we should be in a moral respect, God can be counted upon to make up the difference—Kant says here that such a belief is "already assured to us through reason" (6:120). So, it seems that as long as a particular ecclesiastical faith regards its historical propositions as dispensable, that ecclesiastical faith can be an effective vehicle for pure moral faith. If an ecclesiastical faith regards its historical propositions as essential, however, it will always come into conflict with, and undermine, moral faith. Moral faith has a chance of making use of ecclesiastical faith, provided it can interpret its historical claims by way of a moral hermeneutic; this is why Kant insists in the previous section upon the priority of the moral interpreter of scripture over that of the scriptural scholar. Without it, ecclesiastical faith becomes not a vehicle but an impediment. Nevertheless, Kant insists upon the ultimate dispensability of this vehicle as a necessary consequence of the moral predisposition, proclaiming that religion will gradually be liberated from everything empirical and from all historical statutes, until "at last the pure faith of religion will rule over all, 'so that God may be all in all'" (6:121).

Division Two: Historical representation of the gradual establishment of the dominion of the good principle on earth

Division Two is, mercifully, much less complex than Division One, but no less important. Kant begins Division Two with an interesting claim. He says, first, that we cannot write the history of moral religion, because the development of moral religion is not a "public condition," which is simply to say that an individual human being can only perceive the advance of moral religion within himself, not in others (6:124). This is a point that Kant has insisted upon all along: the disposition, which alone determines moral worth, is inscrutable.

If we want to draw up a history of religion, then, we have to do so with reference to ecclesiastical faith, not moral faith. And we assess the history of ecclesiastical faith by comparing it in its various forms with the pure and immutable religious faith. Pure religious faith, therefore, serves as the standard against which we can judge the progress of ecclesiastical faith (6:124). Indeed, until ecclesiastical faith has a standard by which it can be judged, there is no way to talk about its progress; all the historian can do is register the constant and contingent transformations of individual faiths over time. Of course, if moral religion is not a public condition, then one can no more perceive its emergence within an ecclesiastical faith than one can perceive the disposition of another human being.

So, Kant says that the history of religion begins, properly speaking, from the moment that an ecclesiastical faith "publicly acknowledges its dependence on the restraining conditions of religious faith, and its necessity to conform to it" (6:124); in other words, the distinction between a rational faith and an ecclesiastical faith must be brought to conscious reflection by this ecclesiastical faith, and the resolution of this distinction must become a task of the utmost moral concern (6:124–125). Only then does the universal church begin to take shape and can the history of moral religion be written.

For Kant, this history begins with Christianity, the only ecclesiastical faith to make the promotion of a pure moral faith the primary task. Despite the fact that Christianity develops out of Judaism and indeed counts the Jewish scriptures as its own sacred texts, Kant insists that Judaism has no connection to the history of moral religion itself. It is an ecclesiastical faith bereft of moral content; Christianity, therefore, represents a radical break with Judaism. Kant's characterization (or mischaracterization) of Judaism is indeed unflattering and unfair, but it is more or less consistent with the standard Christian theological assessment of Judaism as well as with philosophical attitudes toward Judaism in the Germany of Kant's time. With that said, let's briefly consider Kant's view of Judaism.

Kant reiterates a view he expressed in Part II: that Judaism originally consisted of the statutory (not moral) laws of a political state—though he concedes that moral laws may later have been appended to it. This means that the Jewish law, in its original form at least, only commanded outward conformity to the law, with no interest in the disposition underlying this conformity. The fact that God was thought to be the author of these laws makes no difference; God was considered as the political leader of the theocracy, and just as secular leaders are concerned with compliance to the law and not with the inner grounds of one's compliance, so too do these divine commands take the form of merely coercive laws (6:125). Even the legislation of the Ten Commandments—a number of which are, in fact, moral laws—are given without any concern for the moral disposition underlying their compliance. Accordingly, the rewards dispensed by God in this world for compliance with these laws are not even dispensed in accordance with ethical concepts; this can be seen from the fact that one's descendants could be punished or rewarded on account of one's compliance (or lack thereof) with the law, which flies in the face of morality (6:126). Kant finds further proof that this legislation is merely statutory in its absence of any reference to a future life. This does not mean that the Jews lacked a conception of a future life; Kant says that they *must* have had an idea of a future life, since belief in it is a part of the universal moral predisposition of human nature (6:126). So, the fact that it is missing can only mean that the lawgiver (represented as God) intentionally did not make reference to it; this indicates that it was his intention to found a political community, not an ethical community. The idea of rewards and punishments in a future life is not proper to a political community, since such rewards and punishments are not within the power of a merely political sovereign.

Finally, Kant notes that Judaism has no place within the history of the universal church precisely because Judaism excludes the rest of humanity from its community and views itself as a people uniquely chosen by God. Even if the God of Judaism is a universal ruler in the sense that he is the creator of all beings, he wills only statutory commands, not moral ones; therefore, this concept of God is not the same concept of God as the one found in moral religion (6:127).

The universal history of the church, then, must begin with the origin of Christianity, which represents rejection and abandonment of the Judaism from which it arose. If the original teachers of this new faith found their own faith prefigured in the Jewish scriptures, this is only because drawing such a connection was the most expedient way to introduce moral religion to the Jews (6:127). Kant does maintain, however, that Christianity's emergence from Judaism was not entirely unprepared; he suggests, as he did in Part II, that Judaism had already been mixed with moral teachings through the influence of Greek philosophy (6:128).

Kant's claim that the history of the church begins with the emergence of Christianity does not, however, constitute a wholesale endorsement of Christianity as a historical faith. On the contrary, he comments that the history of Christianity "has nothing in any way to recommend it" (6:130) and then goes on to provide a list of Christianity's ills. Yet in spite of those ills, it is still apparent that the "true first purpose" of Christianity was the introduction into human history of a pure religious faith. Moreover, the present period in Church history (i.e., *Kant's* present) is the best period in church history, he insists, because the seeds of true religious faith are being openly sown in Christianity, and he expects these seeds to grow "unhindered" in continuous approximation of the church invisible (6:131). Of what, precisely, do these seeds of true religion consist? Kant goes on to say that "in all lands in our part of the world," those who "revere true religion" have adopted two principles universally:

1. *The principle of moderation in claims concerning revelation.* Since it is always possible (though not provable) that a particular scripture that contains moral content may, in fact, be a divine revelation, and since humans cannot easily come together into a single religion unless there is a scripture and an ecclesiastical faith derived from it, it makes perfect sense to use whatever revelation and ecclesiastical faith is already at hand for the promotion of true religion. Therefore, this faith should not be attacked, neither should it be forced upon anyone as though it were required for his salvation (6:132).

2. *The principle that scripture must be interpreted and taught in the interest of morality.* Revelation is adopted by the ecclesiastical faith not to provide for the human being moral maxims that could not have been discovered independently of revelation, but only to give the human being a "vivid presentation" of the idea of "virtue striving toward holiness." Therefore, this revelation must always be taught and interpreted in the interest of morality, with repeated emphasis on the point that true religion does not consist in the knowledge of what God does for our salvation but in what we must do to become worthy of salvation, and further that the only thing that makes us pleasing to God is doing what has unconditional value: moral action (6:132–133).

All of this presupposes, of course, that rulers allow these principles to spread, something that cannot be taken for granted; after all, Kant himself was the victim of a program to censor Enlightenment ideas concerning religion in the name of religious orthodoxy. Kant insists that rulers have a duty not to inhibit the spread of these ideas, and in fact, that it is dangerous to arbitrarily favor certain historical ecclesiastical doctrines by offering benefits or threatening punishment for conformity to these doctrines. Such policies do violence to conscience and the freedom of the subjects of the state is thereby harmed; this freedom is "holy," precisely because it is the necessary condition of moral action, which alone makes one holy. In an important note, Kant responds to the idea that the state cannot do harm to conscience because it only forbids the public declaration of religious opinions but does not prevent anyone from thinking what they wish to think. While the secular power indeed cannot hinder free thought, the spiritual power *can*, and, in fact, it can exercise this coercion even upon the secular power. Ecclesiastical authorities have this power because of the human propensity, discussed earlier, to servile forms of worship, which makes it quite easy for religious authorities to instill in their congregations a terror at deviating from contingent and historical dogmas and practices, and indeed a terror at questioning these dogmas and practices at all. Therefore, while being free from coercion is only a matter of *willing* to be free (at least as far as freedom of thought is concerned), spiritual authorities have the power to place an internal "bar" on this very willing (6:134n).

Kant closes Division Two with a moral interpretation of Christian eschatological representations, that is, representations of the final end and destiny of the world. These representations include the prophecies found, for example, in the Book of Revelation, which depict the arrival of a Kingdom of Heaven. For Kant, such representations are to be taken not as history (or, more precisely, future history known through prophecy) but as the portrayal in historical narrative of the ideal of the arrival of a moral world order, the highest good possible on earth. It is within this framework that all of the elements of these Christian representations of the end of the world must find their proper meaning.

General Remark

Kant's third General Remark concerns "mysteries." In Christian theology, a mystery is a doctrine—divinely revealed and accepted on faith—that transcends human understanding. The paradigmatic example of a mystery in Christian theology is the doctrine of the Trinity. According to this doctrine, God is one, and yet there are three "persons"—Father, Son, and Holy Spirit—in this one God. Each of these three persons is distinct from the other, yet each is identical to God. Clearly, this teaching poses problems for rational thought—how can each of these persons really be distinct, if they are all identical to God? How can God be one, if these three persons are really distinct? Fortunately, these are questions we don't have to answer, and if they turn out to be unanswerable, this is not in itself a problem from the perspective of Christian theology. As a "mystery," the Trinity is something that must be accepted as revealed truth, despite the fact that it transcends human understanding.

Without even reading this General Remark, we can already anticipate that while Kant will not dogmatically deny the truth of any such religious mystery, he will insist both that we cannot claim to have theoretical insight into such supersensible realities and that belief in such mysteries should not be taken as a form of divine service. Yet, in keeping with the goal of making use of Christian representations to express moral ideas, Kant may well wish to put the Christian doctrine of the Trinity to good moral use. This indeed is one of the tasks of this General Remark. The Trinity does not, however, count as a mystery for Kant, as we will see, since the Trinity (on his interpretation) simply gives expression to the idea of God generated by practical reason.

Are there then any such things as "mysteries" for Kant? The answer is yes, though, as expected, he gives his own peculiar definition to this term. Kant defines a mystery as "something *holy*, which can indeed be *cognized* by every individual, yet cannot be *professed* publicly, i.e. cannot be communicated universally" (6:137). When Kant says that a mystery is "holy," he is using the word in the way in which he has been using it throughout the *Religion*, namely, to refer to something *moral*. So for Kant, mysteries pertain to morality and as such, are cognizable. Yet there is an element of this definition that places it decidedly outside of a religion that is within the boundaries of mere reason: a mystery cannot be communicated universally, which is to say that it is something about which we can have no *theoretical* cognition.

What kinds of mysteries does Kant have in mind? He will delineate three mysteries in this General Remark, all of which will be connected to the idea of *freedom*. Freedom itself is not mysterious, since cognition of it is universally communicable: every human being becomes aware of his freedom through the determination of his power of choice by the moral law. The *ground* of our freedom, however, is inscrutable to us, as we have seen in Part I. By "ground," Kant simply means what determines the use of freedom. We cannot account for the use of freedom through natural causality, so we are left with no means to account for, for example, the adoption of an evil or a good disposition. Kant says that when we apply the idea of freedom to the final object of practical reason (our final moral end), we are then led into "holy mysteries." Before looking at these holy mysteries, let's first look at Kant's comments concerning the Trinity.

First of all, Kant says that the task of practical reason is not to determine what God is in himself (in his own nature)—this is a theoretical preoccupation that surpasses the bounds of human reason anyway—but only to determine what God must be to satisfy the needs of practical reason. The idea of God generated by practical reason has three essential features: God is (1) a *holy* lawgiver, (2) a *benevolent* ruler, and (3) a *just* judge. There is nothing mysterious about these three features of God, as they derive from practical reason and can be found, Kant says, in the religions of "most civilized peoples" (6:140). Yet it is Christianity that first purified this faith of all anthropomorphism in the service of moral religion; therefore, its public teaching can, in this respect, be considered as the revelation of a mystery that was previously unknown to the human race. According to this Christian revelation, God as *holy lawgiver* isn't "merciful," "forbearing," or "despotic"; rather, his laws are tied directly to our moral concepts and are directed to the holiness of the human being. As a *benevolent ruler*, God makes up for the human incapacity to live up to the divine holiness, but only on the condition that the human being first makes himself well-pleasing to God through a good moral disposition. Finally, as a *just judge*, God is not lenient, neither does he expect humans to live up to a holiness of which they are not capable. This moral faith in a divine Trinity, Kant says, is a practical idea that finds its reflection in a three-fold division of powers (legislative, executive, and judicial) in a political state. It is, however, *only* a practical idea; the claim that the Trinity gives expression to what God is in himself surpasses the limits of human knowledge, and when understood theoretically rather than practically is unsuitable for the promotion of moral faith.

If *practical* faith in the Trinity is not mysterious, there nevertheless are three mysteries that Kant delineates in this General Remark— things for which there is a practical need, even though their possibility cannot be grasped theoretically.

The mystery of the call

Just as God can only be considered the author of the laws of nature if he is the creator of nature, God can only be considered a moral legislator if he is regarded as the creator of human beings. But, Kant asks, how can a *created* being act *freely*? The principle of causality, according to Kant, says that we cannot attribute any other inner ground of action in created beings (humans) than what the producing cause (God) has placed in them. But if God has placed this inner ground of action in human beings, then it would seem impossible for human actions to really be free; human freedom seems impossible to reconcile with the concept of creation. Rather than thinking of ourselves as created beings, then, Kant says that we must think of ourselves as *already existing* free beings determined to citizenship in God's kingdom not by virtue of having been *created* by God but by virtue of having been *called* by God. The idea that we are beings called to citizenship in God's kingdom is, practically speaking, quite clear, but exactly how it is that humans can be so called is something into which we can have no insight and is, therefore, an impenetrable mystery. Ultimately, this mystery of the call is nothing other than the mystery of morality that we have spoken of previously: how is it that natural beings can break with natural causality to respond to the unconditional call of the moral law?

The mystery of satisfaction

The human being, as far as we can tell, is corrupted and inadequate to the holy law, and he has no way of compensating for this inadequacy on his own. If indeed the human being is called to God's kingdom, there must be some way of making up for this deficiency. Yet reason tells us that all human goodness must stem from the human being's own use of freedom. We must assume, therefore, that God has a means of compensating for human inadequacy—and yet precisely *how* compensation can be made and yet have *moral* worth for the human being is an impenetrable mystery.

The mystery of election

Even if we allow that such satisfaction for the lack of human holiness is possible, a "morally believing acceptance" of this assistance is itself a "determination of the will toward the good," which already presupposes a disposition well-pleasing to God. In other words, on a moral understanding of satisfaction, the human being must first make himself good in order to become worthy of this satisfaction. But how could the human being have attained this disposition on his own, given his corruption? It must be the result of God's grace. Why such grace should be granted to one and yet denied to another, not on account of their works but on account of some inscrutable divine decree—and moreover, how all of this could be compatible with divine justice—is a mystery.

Kant's remarks concerning the mystery of election are a bit enigmatic at first glance; isn't the notion of a divine decree entirely incompatible with moral religion? Yet his meaning can, I think, be clarified by looking at a footnote from earlier in Part III, in which he comments on Romans 9.18, the text in which the apostle Paul says that God "has mercy on whomever he wills, and he hardens whomever he wills." This verse can, and has been, interpreted to mean that God predestines humans to salvation or damnation. It goes without saying that such an interpretation would be morally unacceptable for Kant. So in this note, he provides an ethical interpretation, saying that it often seems to us that the predispositions that make one human being good and another bad are already present from birth, and that "contingencies of life" that no one can control often appear to be the decisive factor in determining why one person becomes good and another evil. So, our inability to say for certain why some become good and others evil is expressed in this line from Romans *as if* God has pronounced a decree concerning the fate of humans before he created them (6:122n). When Kant speaks of election here, he is not referring to an actual divine decree but is simply expressing the mystery that we run up against when we try to account for the moral destiny of individual people, and moreover the mystery that we face when we try to explain how the contingencies of life that seem to shape our moral dispositions can be reconciled with the freedom that must be presupposed for moral imputation.

Concerning these three mysteries, Kant says that God has revealed nothing. And if he did, we could not understand it, because humans cannot have insight into the "causes" that give rise to free action. God has left in obscurity the causes whereby free action occurs or does not occur. Regarding the objective rule of our conduct, however, everything we need is revealed through reason and scripture, and every human being is capable of understanding it. It would be presumptuous to require that more than this be revealed to us (6:144–145).

Part IV: Concerning service and counterfeit service under the dominion of the good principle, or, of religion and priestcraft

As we have seen, the struggle against evil is not a strictly individual affair, given the tendency of humans to corrupt one another. For this reason, the process of restoration to the good involves both a prototype of a human being well-pleasing to God (Part II) and a prototype of an ethical community, which Kant calls the "church" (Part III). Both prototypes are ideas generated by human reason independently of historically revealed religion, but historically revealed religion is capable of giving sensible expression to these moral ideas, thereby serving as a vehicle for the promotion of pure moral religion. Yet revealed religion is a double-edged sword; it is also capable of subverting morality, and it does so in regular and predictable ways.

In the first part of Part IV, Kant shows how revealed religion can work in the service of the good by examining a particular example of a historical faith that has morality at its core: Christianity. Kant builds his case that Christianity is a "natural religion" through an examination of Jesus' teachings, particularly those found in the Sermon on the Mount. He then examines Christianity as a "learned religion," whose authority comes not from reason but from historical demonstration. Then in the second part of Part IV, Kant diagnoses how historical faiths go wrong, resulting in "religious delusion," "fetishism," "counterfeit service," and "priestcraft."

First part: Concerning the service of God in a religion in general

Kant's first order of business (after a brief recapitulation of the ideas found in Part III) is to define the word "religion." As we have seen, Kant distinguishes in Part III between "religion" and "faith," claiming that there is only one religion, though there can be many faiths (Jewish, Christian, Islamic, etc.). However common it might be to speak of multiple "religions," Kant insists that this word be reserved for true, moral religion, which is always one and the same wherever it is found (6:107–108).

Here in Part IV, Kant defines religion, "subjectively considered," as "the recognition of all our duties as divine commands" (6:153–154). He saves the explication of this definition for a lengthy footnote, and in the main text, immediately proceeds to subdivide religion into two forms, "revealed" and "natural." In revealed religion, one must first know that something is a divine command before recognizing it as a duty; in natural religion, one must first know that something is a duty before recognizing it as a divine command (6:154). So, the word "religion" generally posits an identity between duties and divine commands; this is what natural and revealed religion have in common. They differ, however, in which of the two elements—duties or divine commands—grounds and makes possible the identification of the other element.

Kant's footnote to his definition of religion merits careful consideration. He says that his definition of religion obviates some "erroneous interpretations" of religion, and he discusses two such interpretations. The first false interpretation that this definition dispels is that religion requires "assertoric knowledge" of supersensible objects, including the existence of God. By assertoric knowledge, Kant means knowledge of the existence (or nonexistence) of something. As we know, Kant does not believe that assertoric knowledge of supersensible objects is possible for human beings; so it is fortunate that religion does not require it. Religion requires not assertoric knowledge but assertoric *faith*, the belief that God exists. Faith in the existence of God does not require knowledge that he exists—if one had such knowledge, faith wouldn't be necessary—but it does require the assumption that it is *possible* for God to exist. Fortunately, Kant takes his critical philosophy to have demonstrated that God's existence cannot be disproven; the denial of God's existence is for Kant as dogmatic a violation of the limits of possible human knowledge as is the affirmation of God's existence (on speculative grounds, at least). It is important to keep in mind, however, that religion is not simply the belief that God is *possible*; as an *assertoric* faith, it is the belief that God actually exists. As an assertoric *faith*, it does not require the actual existence of God but simply the idea of God (6:154), and since this idea of God is derived from practical (not speculative) reason, it is the idea of a *moral* God.

The second misunderstanding that this definition of religion obviates, Kant says, is the idea that religion is the "aggregate of *particular* duties immediately relating to God" (6:154). In any universal religion—and remember that Kant reserves the word religion strictly for universal religion—there can be no particular duties owed to God, since God "cannot receive anything from us." Thus, Kant says, this definition precludes any attempts to win God's favor through works of "courtly service"; all that God requires, in accordance with this idea of God, is the performance of the ethico-civil duties we have toward ourselves and other human beings (ibid.).

After distinguishing between revealed and natural religion, Kant distinguishes between *rationalists* and *supernaturalists* in matters of faith. The supernaturalist is a partisan of revealed religion; he maintains that universal religion requires faith in divine revelation. The rationalist, by contrast, believes that natural religion alone is required for universal religion. Kant divides the rationalist into two further types: the *naturalist*, who denies the existence of any supernatural divine revelation; and the *pure rationalist*, who allows the possibility of divine revelation but does not believe that it is necessary to recognize or accept it for universal religion. But no sooner does Kant introduce this distinction between two different kinds of rationalists than he revokes the naturalist's "rationalist" credentials, since the naturalist transgresses the boundaries of human knowledge by categorically denying the possibility of divine revelation. The real distinction in play, then, is between the supernaturalist and the pure rationalist (6:154–155).

The division between natural and revealed religion is a division of religion "according to its first origin and inner possibility," but religion can also be divided according to "the characteristic that renders it capable of *external communication*" (6:155). Here, Kant is raising the question of how a person can be convinced of the truth of religion and therefore how religion can be transmitted from one person or one generation to another. He says that there are two different means of communication. Religion that convinces strictly on the basis of reason is "natural religion"; religion that convinces only by means of erudition is called "learned religion." Only natural religion is, according to Kant, "universally communicable," and therefore, it alone can be universally binding (6:155).

But what exactly does Kant mean by "erudition"? A learned religion contains dogmas that cannot be known through reason, and so, these dogmas must come to be known some other way. Initially, when these dogmas are first revealed, they are typically accompanied by miracles and wonders that convince those present of the authority and veracity of these revelations; such is the case in Christianity, in which Jesus' teachings are accompanied and authenticated by miracles. But unless there is a "continuous miracle of revelation," Kant says, at a certain point these revelations must be documented and written down for posterity; these written documents become the sacred trust of the learned. These sacred writings are essentially historical documents, and therefore, historical authentication is required for people to be convinced of their truth. Erudition, then, refers to the body of knowledge possessed by the learned in order to authenticate and properly explicate these sacred writings. This requires knowledge of the original language of scripture, as well as a wide body of historical knowledge, and therefore, the "unlearned"—who must rely upon translations of these scriptures and do not possess the requisite historical learning—depend upon the learned. As Kant noted in Part III, an ecclesiastical faith is ultimately "just a faith in scholars" (6:114).

Kant's major claim here in the first part of Part IV is that Christianity is a religion that is both natural and learned. Such a hybrid religion is possible, Kant says, if this religion is such that people could (and should) have arrived at it through the use of their own reason, and yet would not have arrived at it as quickly or as thoroughly were it not for the historical revelation that introduced it and made it publicly known. Such a religion is *objectively* a natural religion but *subjectively* a revealed one. Given that Kant sees revealed religion always and only as a means to the end of natural religion, he says that the supernatural revelation can be forgotten entirely without the hybrid religion losing anything truly essential; by contrast, if the supernatural revelation of a purely learned religion were to be lost or forgotten, the religion would itself disappear from the world (6:155–156).

Kant's task, then, is to consider Christianity first as a natural religion and then as a learned religion. To determine whether a particular religion is natural, one must investigate its scriptures—in this case, the New Testament—to see whether the teachings found there are ethical and therefore rational. Kant believes that the core of the New Testament consists of ethical teachings. In his account of these teachings, Kant relies almost entirely on the Sermon on the Mount (Mt. 5-7). Jesus, Kant says, teaches the following:

1. Only a pure moral disposition can make a human well-pleasing to God, not the fulfillment of any statutory ecclesiastical duties (Mt. 5.20-48).
2. Sinning in thought is equivalent to sinning in deed (Mt. 5.28).
3. Holiness is the goal for which human beings should strive (Mt. 5.48).
4. Hating in one's heart is tantamount to killing (Mt. 5.22).
5. An injustice done to one's neighbor cannot be made right through acts of divine service, but only by rendering satisfaction to the neighbor himself (Mt. 5.24).
6. Oaths detract from respect for the truth itself (Mt. 5.34-37).
7. The evil propensity of the human heart must be reversed such that the desire for revenge is transformed into tolerance (Mt. 5.39-40), and hatred of one's enemies into beneficence (Mt. 5.44).
8. Through the idea of the straight gate and narrow way, Jesus teaches against the misinterpretation of the law that would consist in the attempt to evade moral duty and make up for it by fulfilling ecclesiastical duty (Mt. 7.13).
9. Jesus requires that the pure moral disposition also be demonstrated in deeds (Mt. 5.16), and rebuffs the hope of those who would attempt to ingratiate themselves into God's favor through invocation and praise in order to make up for a lack of deeds.
10. Jesus insists that these deeds be performed publicly as an example for imitation (Mt. 5.16), not as though one were being forced to perform them, but cheerfully (Mt. 5.16), so that from a small beginning religion will gradually grow into a veritable kingdom of God (Mt. 13.31-33).

Kant then notes that Jesus sums up these duties into a *universal* rule and a *particular* rule. The universal rule is to "do your duty from no other incentive except the unmediated appreciation of duty itself; i.e. love God (the Legislator of all duties) above all else"; the particular rule is to "love every one as yourself, i.e. promote his welfare from an unmediated good-will, one not derived from selfish incentives" (6:160–161). Finally, concerning the hope of future reward, Jesus promises reward strictly proportioned to virtue, that is, different rewards in accordance with the different dispositions with which one sacrifices happiness in this world for the sake of moral conduct (6:161). This, Kant says, is a complete religion that can be proposed to each human being through his own reason (6:162).

There is some irony in the fact that the Gospel of Matthew—which furnishes most of the evidence for Kant's claim that Christianity is a natural religion—is in many ways the most "Jewish" of the four gospels, insofar as the Jesus of Matthew seems least inclined to dismiss what Kant would consider the merely "statutory" elements of Judaism. It is Matthew's Jesus, after all, who proclaims that "until heaven and earth pass away, not an iota, not a dot, will pass from the Law until all is accomplished" (5:18).

Yet Kant is aware of the presence of Jewish elements in the Gospels, elements that he must account for in some way, given his thoroughgoing denunciation of Judaism as merely statutory. And he does so by appealing yet again to the means-end logic that is so characteristic of the *Religion*. The appeals to Jewish legislation found in the New Testament—and, for that matter, the claim that the New Testament is prefigured and therefore validated by the Old Testament—are only utilized for the sake of introducing Jesus' new moral teachings "among people who, without exception and blindly, clung to the old" (6:162). And in his discussion of Christianity as a learned religion, Kant praises this decision on the part of the "first founders of *congregations*" to intertwine these teachings with the history of Judaism. (Note that he does *not* attribute this decision to the "first teacher," but only to the first founders of congregations; and the founders of the *church* will betray the intention of these founders of congregations by taking for essential articles of faith statutes introduced merely as a means.) This decision was sound, however, "only perhaps with respect to that situation," the implication of course being that continued reliance on the teachings and texts of Judaism is no longer sound. In a note, in fact, Kant voices concern that continued profession of faith in the sacred history recounted in the Old Testament is an "onerous burden" for the "conscientious" (6:167n). This is because he does not feel that the Old Testament can, on account of its antiquity, be brought to the same level of historical credibility as that of the New Testament (6:166). This is not to say that Christianity, as a learned religion, does not suffer from some of the same problems as Judaism in this respect; Kant notes that the authentication of the events recounted in the Christian scriptures must make do without the corroboration of contemporaries. But this is not an insurmountable problem because Christianity has an advantage over Judaism: the teachings proclaimed by its first teacher constitute a moral rather than statutory religion; and since these teachings are rational, they can be propagated and authenticated even in the absence of historical scholarship (6:167).

Second part: Concerning the counterfeit service of God in a statutory religion

Christianity, of course, has a history beyond the time of Jesus and the first founders of the Christian congregations, and Kant understands this history to be in many ways the history of a betrayal of the principles of the first teacher. In the first part, Kant has argued that Christianity is both natural and revealed, and that the revealed elements of Christianity are just a vehicle for the transmission of natural religion; in the second part, he will examine the ways in which this vehicle undermines true religion rather than promoting it, plunging Christianity back into statutory religion and what Kant calls "counterfeit service of God."

"Counterfeit service" is one of four interrelated terms that Kant employs in Part IV to analyze the subversion of natural religion by revealed religion; the others are "religious delusion," "fetishism," and "priestcraft." We will consider these four terms before examining the issue of "conscience," with which Kant closes Part IV.

Counterfeit service, Kant says, consists in acting upon a religious delusion (6:168), so we will begin by considering the meaning of religious delusion. Kant defines "delusion" generally as "the mistake of regarding the mere representation of a thing as equivalent to the thing itself" (6:168n). In this footnote, Kant delineates different forms of delusion: for example, the delusion called "madness" consists in taking the representations of one's imagination for the things themselves. Other forms of delusion—which Kant classifies as "practical delusions"—consist not in taking a representation of a thing for the thing itself, but rather in regarding the possession of something that is merely a means to an end as possession of the end itself. Religious delusion is precisely a practical delusion in this sense: it consists in taking statutory faith—which Kant insists is *merely a means* to further the end of true moral religion—as the end in itself and therefore as essential and indispensable to the service of God (ibid.). In other words, religious delusion consists in the belief that statutory religion is the *true* religion. Once this delusion of taking the means for the end results in the performance of acts believed to constitute genuine service of God, one is engaged in counterfeit service.

What is the source of religious delusion? Or, as Kant asks, what is the "universal subjective ground" of religious delusion, the tendency of human beings to substitute means for end in religious matters? Kant says that, seeing as we make a God for ourselves, it is natural that we should make him in whatever way is most advantageous to us, sparing ourselves the exertion of having to improve our moral dispositions (6:168–169). Lest the reader balk at the idea of humans "making" a God for themselves, Kant clarifies his meaning in a footnote added to the second edition. He writes that in order to recognize a being as "God"—a being described in scripture, for example, or even one that miraculously appears to a person directly—one must have first formed a concept of God against which to compare it; otherwise, there is no way to know whether the being that one reveres is truly God, and one, thus, risks falling into "idolatry," the worship of a false God (6:169n). To ensure the worship of the true God, then, humans must first construct a concept of God to serve as the true measure against which any claimants can be judged. But this leaves open the possibility, and indeed the likelihood, that humans will construct a God very much in their own image. While such anthropomorphism is unavoidable—how could humans possibly represent a supersensible being if not anthropomorphically?—it is dangerous when we conceive of the divine will and his *relationship to morality* in all-too-human terms (6:168–169).

Kant insists repeatedly in the *Religion* that the only service that the true God requires is moral action; so how can one account for the tendency of human beings to form for themselves a "God" who requires other forms of service? Kant's answer is essentially that given by Hume in *The Natural History of Religion* (1757). Hume laments the fact that "in every religion, however sublime the verbal definition which it gives of its divinity, many of the votaries, perhaps the greatest number, will still seek the divine favour, not by virtue and good morals, which alone can be acceptable to a perfect being, but either by frivolous observances, by intemperate zeal, by rapturous extasies [sic], or by the belief of mysterious and absurd opinions" (Section XIV). Indeed, so obstinate are people in this belief, that if a religion were ever to be found in which the priests consistently preach in their sermons that God favors moral behavior alone, the people would "make the very attendance on these sermons the essentials of religion, rather than place them in virtue and good morals" (ibid.). And when Hume attempts to account for this tendency, his explanation is precisely the same as Kant's account of the universal subjective ground of religious delusion. When it comes to moral duty, Hume says, the human being feels that this is something he owes to himself and others, and that in discharging this duty, there is no particular service to the deity by which he can win divine favor.

> And any practice, recommended to him, which either serves to no purpose in life, or offers the strongest violence to his natural inclinations; that practice he will the more readily embrace, on account of those very circumstances which should make him absolutely reject it. . . . In restoring a loan, or paying a debt, his divinity is nowise beholden to him; because these acts of justice are what he was bound to perform, and what many would have performed, were there no God in the universe. But if he fast a day, or give himself a sound whipping; this has a direct reference, in his opinion, to the service of God. No other motive could engage him to such austerities. By these distinguished marks of devotion, he has now acquired the divine favour; and may expect, in recompense, protection and safety in this world, and eternal happiness in the next. (Section XIV)

For Kant as well, humans reason according to a principle which says that only those things done for the sake of pleasing God demonstrate our obedience to him; and various forms of self-sacrifice have, therefore, always been taken to be an extremely potent means with which to win divine favor, precisely on account of their *uselessness*:

"The more useless such self-inflicted torments are, the less aimed at the universal moral improvement of the human being, the holier they seem to be. For, just because they have absolutely no use in the world, and yet cost effort, they seem to be aimed solely at attesting devotion to God" (6:169). All of this constitutes religious delusion, Kant concludes. This behavior demonstrates our eagerness to take on an attitude of devotion or dedication to God, even though it is not, in fact, true devotion. But the devotee takes this mere attitude of readiness—which, in itself, is only valuable as the *means* to true devotion—as though it were devotion itself.

Against this religious delusion, Kant formulates the "moral principle of religion": "*Apart from a good-life conduct, anything which the human being supposes that he can do to become well-pleasing to God is mere religious delusion and counterfeit service of God*" (6:170–171). Kant says that this is a principle "requiring no proof"; and indeed it seems not to require any proof, assuming that Kant is correct in his belief that natural religion requires so little capacity for theoretical reason that every human being can be convinced of it (6:157).

Kant's denial that there is anything other than good life conduct that humans can do to become pleasing to God does *not* amount to a denial, he says, that there might be something that *God* can do, above and beyond our good life conduct, to make us well-pleasing to him. However, for a church to proclaim as revealed truth that God has, in fact, done some such thing, and further to proclaim that belief in, and profession of, this revealed truth itself is necessary to become well-pleasing to God—*that*, says Kant, constitutes religious delusion. In fact, making a profession of faith the condition of becoming well-pleasing to God is worse than requiring any of the other superfluous works that statutory religions so frequently require, since it pressures a person to declare something contrary to his conscience. Kant will have more to say about conscience at the end of Part IV.

Let us proceed now to "fetishism" and "priestcraft." Kant begins Section 3 (6:175–185) with the claim—again following Hume's *Natural History of Religion*—that the worship of mighty invisible beings was "wrung from the helpless human being because of the fear naturally rooted in the consciousness of his powerlessness" (6:175–176). Kant does not pursue this line of inquiry much further (unlike Hume, who attempts to give an entirely naturalistic account of religion), except to say that this first veneration of mighty invisible beings does not count as religion but mere "servile worship." The public form of this servile worship, with its attendant laws, Kant calls "temple service." It is only when these laws become associated with the "moral culture of human beings" that this temple service becomes "ecclesiastical service." But both temple service and ecclesiastical service are merely historical forms of faith, that is, until ecclesiastical faith as a provisional means gives itself over to pure (nonhistorical) religious faith. But with regard to the historical (nonmoral) elements of divine service themselves, there is no difference in principle between them, however "refined" or "primitive" they might appear; as Kant says, "between the wholly sensuous *Wogulite*, who in the morning lays the paw of a bear skin over his head with the short prayer, 'Strike me not dead!' and the sublimated *Puritan* and Independent in Connecticut, there certainly is a tremendous distance in the *style* of faith, but not in the *principle*" (6:176). Both the Wogulite and the Puritan try to control mighty invisible beings; they simply employ different methods to accomplish that goal.

"Fetishism," for Kant, denotes the attempt to employ a natural means to produce supernatural effects, for which the term "sorcery" is usually applied, though Kant uses fetishism instead to avoid the attendant concept of "commerce with the evil principle" (6:177). Any human actions that contain no moral value and yet are performed with the hope of winning God's favor fall under the category of fetishism. (Kant will also discuss the idea of using a natural means to produce a supernatural effect in the General Remark to Part IV, which deals with the "means of grace.")

"Priestcraft" (*Pfaffentum*) designates the constitution of a church insofar as its operating principle is fetishistic (6:179). In a second edition note, Kant claims not to be singling out any one particular sect (Catholicism) with this term but only designating "spiritual despotism" wherever it might be found (6:176n). But what exactly is the connection between fetish-service and spiritual despotism? The human being imposes moral laws upon himself through his own reason, and therefore, he takes the burden of these laws upon himself freely—this is the meaning that Kant finds in Jesus' saying (Mt. 11.30), "For my yoke is easy, and my burden is light" (6:179n). However, fetishism requires the human being to believe in something that can only be known historically and that therefore cannot command universal conviction. Fetishism is, thus, coercive, and burdens the conscience (6:179). Whatever forms the actual constitution of a fetishistic church may take (monarchic, aristocratic, or democratic), it is always "despotic," since it imposes submission to its statutes. Since the priests or clergy act as the "single authoritative guardian and interpreter of the will of the invisible lawgiver," they are, therefore, able to dispense with reason and scriptural scholarship entirely. Thus fetishism, for Kant, inevitably involves "spiritual despotism" and moreover leads to the clergy's usurpation of authority from the state, given the influence it has over the minds of its citizens (6:180).

Religious delusion, counterfeit service, fetishism, and priestcraft—all of this is the result, Kant says, of the seemingly "harmless transposition" of means and ends. Indeed, Kant says that *enlightenment* consists precisely in combining two "good things" (means and ends) in the proper order (6:180). The enlightenment to which Kant calls human beings through the proper ordering of means and ends is not an enlightenment intended only for the learned or those skilled at reasoning; the whole human race, "even the ignorant, or those most limited conceptually," are called to it. It might seem, Kant concedes, that a historical faith, with its anthropomorphic God and sensible representations, requiring mere assent to simple narratives and little actual understanding, would be best suited to the unlearned, better so than moral faith. But in fact, there is a practical cognition so close and accessible to even the simplest human being that it seems "as though it had been literally inscribed in his heart"—the unconditional binding force of the moral law. This cognition either leads to faith in God directly or else shapes the concept of God into that of a moral legislator. A pure moral faith can be easily elicited from the unlearned, and therefore, it is not only prudent to begin with moral rather than historical faith, but also a duty to make it the condition for the hope of partaking in whatever salvation might be promised by a historical faith (6:181–182).

Kant closes the main body of Part IV (before the General Remark) with some important remarks on conscience (§4). What exactly is conscience? Kant says that it is a moral principle requiring no proof that one should not perform an action where there is danger that one's action might be morally wrong. One is obligated, therefore, to investigate the rightness or wrongness of one's proposed actions. It is reason, Kant says, that judges whether a particular action is right or wrong. Conscience, however, is not reason's judgment of the rightness or wrongness of an action, but rather reason's *judgment of itself* to determine whether it has, in fact, scrupulously examined the rightness or wrongness of a proposed action. In other words, conscience is a form of self-examination to determine whether one has done one's due diligence in investigating the morality of one's actions. If one has done one's due diligence, then one can be said to act according to conscience; if not, then one is guilty of *lack of conscience* (6:185–186).

Kant wants to see how conscience so defined can serve as a "guiding thread" in matters of faith, as the title of Section 4 indicates, and more specifically, how it can serve as the basis of a critique of persecution for unbelief and commanded professions of faith. Kant considers the case of an inquisitor who condemns an otherwise upstanding citizen to death for unbelief. This inquisitor truly believes in the exclusive truth of his particular statutory faith, and believes, moreover, that God has given him permission and indeed required him to root out unbelief and unbelievers. Kant believes, of course, that the inquisitor has acted immorally; this is not the question that he wishes to address here. Kant's question, rather, is whether the inquisitor has simply made an error in judgment and is innocent of wrongdoing insofar as he acted according to his conscience, or whether he is guilty of a *lack* of conscience.

Kant begins his argument that the inquisitor is guilty of a lack of conscience by claiming that it is certainly a moral wrong for the inquisitor to take the life of a human being unless God decrees otherwise and makes his will known to the inquisitor in some way. (We should understand Kant to be making this claim simply for the sake of argument, since he would discount the possibility that God, who wills in accordance with the moral law, could make such a decree in the first place.) Can the inquisitor be sure, beyond a shadow of a doubt, that God has, in fact, made this decree? If this revelation came to him through the intermediary of other human beings (as it would if the inquisitor believed God's command to be given in scripture), error on this matter would certainly be possible. In fact, Kant says, even if this command came to him directly, as it allegedly came to Abraham when God ordered him to sacrifice his son Isaac, error is possible; Kant does not explain why error is possible here, though presumably one who receives such a direct revelation would have to at least admit the possibility of hallucination, mental illness, or less naturalistically, the possibility that this miraculous experience was demonic rather than theistic. Of course, in Kant's earlier reference to the story of the binding of Isaac in the General Remark to Part II, Kant categorically rejects the possibility that God could issue such a command by employing his "negative criterion" for determining whether some miraculous event (like a direct revelation) comes from God: "if something is represented as commanded by God in a direct manifestation of him yet is directly in conflict with morality, it cannot be a divine miracle despite every appearance of being one" (6:87). In any case, Kant's point here is that in every "historical or phenomenal faith," there is always the possibility of error. The inquisitor, therefore, cannot have truly done his due diligence in determining his certitude in the rightness of his action and is guilty, therefore, of a lack of conscience.

Since acting according to conscience is a moral duty, any religious authority that commands a sincere profession of faith in articles grounded on historical proofs alone (which can never be entirely certain) is guilty of wrongdoing (6:187). So too is the person who attempts to play it safe by professing belief in doctrines that he knows cannot be professed with complete certainty (6:188–189). The "true maxim of safety," Kant says, consists in the recognition that while one can never be certain that historical faith is true, neither can one be sure that it is not true (provided it does not conflict with morality), and in the assurance that whatever benefit might come from this historical faith will come to the believer so long as he makes himself worthy of it through good life conduct (6:189). Kant concludes by suggesting (rather optimistically) that every author of a creed and teacher of a church would "quake" at the following question, if only he would pose it to himself: would he dare to profess his own certainty in the truth of his propositions in the sight of God, who sees his sincerity clearly, on pain of losing everything that he holds dear? If he would indeed quake at this question, then it cannot be consistent with conscientiousness to insist that anyone make a profession of faith, or to make such faith into a duty and a form of divine service (6:189–190).

General Remark

This fourth General Remark, Kant says, could bear the title "Means of Grace" (6:52), which refers to the human's attempt to influence the supernatural and draw down God's grace upon himself through his natural actions. "Means of grace," then, can be distinguished from "effects of grace" (discussed in the first General Remark), insofar as effects of grace concern supernatural influences that we receive *passively*.

Recall that by grace, Kant means what God does for us to make us morally better and well-pleasing to him, as opposed to what we do for ourselves. Since grace is, by definition, supernatural, human reason does not have any insight into whether there is, in fact, any such thing as grace, and if there is, how, when, or to what extent it exerts an influence upon us (6:191). Moreover, the idea of grace is difficult to reconcile with the fact that any moral good attributed to us must result from the use of our own free powers. Is there a way for supernatural influence to act in concert with our freedom, such that divine assistance can make us *morally better* human beings? Kant does not rule this out as impossible, since we are ultimately as ignorant about the operations of human freedom as we are of divine grace; after all, both grace and freedom, assuming they both exist, produce effects in the natural world and yet are distinct from natural causality. In any case, Kant's basic attitude toward the idea of grace is this: the human being can reasonably presuppose that, if he uses his freedom to the fullest possible extent to make himself into the human being he ought to be, then—and only then—God will supply whatever else might be necessary to make that human being well-pleasing to him. Beyond this general supposition, we can make no further use of the idea of grace (ibid.).

With this in mind, let us consider what Kant says about "means of grace." First of all, Kant reminds us of a point that he has made a number of times in the *Religion*: humans need to give sensible representation to moral ideas. True moral service of God, Kant says, is invisible, since it consists simply in the disposition—itself invisible—of obedience to all true moral duties as divine commands (6:192). Yet humans have a need to represent this invisible service of God in visible form. Such visible representation can indeed be useful as a means for the cultivation of true (invisible) service of God, particularly, as Kant said in Part III, when moral religion is being first introduced to people who have hitherto been practicing a merely *statutory* religion (6:109). The danger, of course, is that human beings take these visible representations not as a *means* for the cultivation of true invisible service of God but as the *end*—a substitution that Kant calls, as we've seen, religious delusion. As with all religious delusion, it is no simple mistaken substitution of means for ends but an "escape route" by which the sensuous human being seeks to circumvent the rigorous demands of morality, convincing himself that God will accept the actions in place of moral striving (6:193).

The idea of a means of grace is, for Kant, a form of delusory faith through which we believe ourselves able to bring about a supernatural effect (God's influence upon our morality) through a purely natural means. It is, thus, identical to fetishism. Kant addresses four such means of grace in this General Remark: (1) praying, (2) church-going, (3) baptism, and (4) communion. Of course, these are only delusory when taken as ends in themselves: properly construed, they all serve as a means for the promotion of true moral service of God. What Kant attempts to do here, then, is to reject the delusory use of these activities and recover their proper moral and edifying functions, either for the individual in his personal path to moral perfection or for humans collectively on the path to realizing an ethical kingdom of God on earth. We will discuss each of them in turn.

1 Praying

For Kant, there is something absurd about the belief that we can bring about God's assistance through prayer. If praying consists in simply declaring a wish to God, it is superfluous, since God sees our inmost thoughts and desires and therefore does not require any such declaration. Understood in this way, prayer accomplishes nothing and does not "serve" God, spuriously or otherwise (6:194). Rather, the "true spirit of prayer," for Kant, is a disposition accompanying all of our actions to perform them as if they are, by their very morality, in the service of God. In this sense, prayer is not something that happens periodically. Instead, Kant says—drawing on the language of scripture (1 Thess. 5.17)—that such prayer is done "without ceasing" (6:195).

True prayer—the disposition to perform all our actions as if they were in the service of God—can be "clothed" in formulas and words that can serve as a means to stimulate this disposition in us (6:195); this clothing is the sensible representation of invisible service of God that, Kant says, sensible beings require. But it is a religious delusion to take these words and formulas not as a means to stimulate the disposition of true service, but rather as forms of service in themselves that work upon God rather than upon us. According to Kant's understanding of prayer, prayer can be sincere even in the absence of certitude in God's existence, precisely because its goal is not to bring about a supernatural effect—which, of course, presupposes that God actually exists—but rather to strengthen our own moral dispositions (6:195n).

In the footnote on prayer added to the second edition of the *Religion*, Kant interprets the Lord's Prayer—the prayer that Jesus instructs his disciples to pray in the Sermon on the Mount (Mt. 6.9-13)—as a verbal expression of the resolution to good life conduct, combined with the "standing wish," in view of our frailty, to become worthy members of God's kingdom. As such, this prayer does not, on Kant's reading, contain any actual request from God; rather, the prayer itself, assuming it is sincere, can bring about its own objective of moral improvement and worthiness of membership in God's kingdom (6:195). As the human being purifies his moral disposition, the spirit of prayer will suffice and the "letter"—the words and formulas that give sensible representation to this spirit of prayer—can pass away, like all other sensible religious representations (6:197).

2 Church-going

Just as the human being's individual moral striving for his own ethical perfection is to be accompanied by the collective endeavor to build an ethical community, so too is prayer to be accompanied by the external worship of God. The true purpose of church-going is to propagate moral goodness; the means to this end is a "sensuous display" of external worship of God. This external worship can and does take various forms, though Kant says that any formalities that could lead to idolatry and thus "burden the conscience" should be avoided. Kant singles out "certain forms of adoration of God personified as infinite goodness under the name of a human being," since such "sensuous portrayal" of God is contrary to the command of reason—which also happens to be a biblical command (Exod. 20.4)—not to make any graven images of God (6:198–199). Kant is a bit vague here, but he seems to be referring to depictions of Jesus and the veneration of such images. In any case, Kant makes the very same point about church-going as he does about prayer: when church-going is employed as a means of grace, as though the very act of performing the various formalities of external worship of God constitutes a meritorious service of God, it is religious delusion (6:199).

3 Baptism

"Baptism" is the initiation of a person into a church, and it either imposes serious moral obligations upon the initiate (if he is an adult) or (in the case of infant baptism) upon the members of the church charged with the initiate's education into the faith. The true purpose of baptism is a holy one: the "formation of a human being as a citizen in a divine state"; but the procedure of baptism does not itself, as a means of grace, confer holiness. To believe that baptism is able to "wash away all sins at once" is for Kant a delusion that openly shows its ties to "pagan superstition" (6:199).

4 Communion

"Communion" is a ritual that serves to continue, renew, and further propagate the church, and to affirm the equality of its members. Kant endorses the Christian ritual of a common meal at the same table as a practice with the power to combat human narrowness, selfishness, and intolerance, instilling a spirit of brotherly love. Yet, once again, the idea that communion is in itself a means to secure God's grace is religious delusion. And given that clergy controls the administration of the communal meal, this particular religious delusion blatantly demonstrates the spiritual despotism of priestcraft (6:199–200).

Kant concludes this General Remark, and indeed the *Religion* as a whole, with the observation that all religious self-deceptions have a common ground: the appeal to God's *mercy* in order to avoid the strenuous work of conforming to God's *holiness*. It is hard work to be a "good servant" through moral duty, but much easier to be one of God's "favorites" whose sins are easily forgiven or at least easily paid for through the intercession of someone more favored still. But this requires a concept of God much diminished from the holy and just God of practical reason; the God who would be complicit in such a scheme is rather modeled upon human rulers, among whose faults are a failure to always dispense grace only where truly merited. Only on the basis of such an anthropomorphic conception of God could a human being plausibly believe that he can win God's favor through formalities and observances by which he shows his devotion to God, all the while failing to do the one thing that can truly win God's favor: making himself a better person. Such a person occupies himself with piety rather than virtue, whereas a genuine religious disposition consists of virtue combined with piety. Should this delusion take a firm hold, a person might then succumb to enthusiasm, believing that he feels the effects of God's grace within himself, and perhaps attaining such "familiarity" with God that virtue itself seems beneath him (6:200–201). True religious devotion belongs, rather, to the simple, honest people "who can be relied upon in daily affairs, in business and in need," and who prove by their example that "the right way to advance is not from grace to virtue but rather from virtue to grace" (6:201–202).

CHAPTER FOUR

Reception and influence

In a sense, the reception of Kant's *Religion* began before he wrote it. In the spring of 1792, a book entitled *Attempt at a Critique of All Revelation* appeared. For some unknown reason, the publisher left the author's name and preface out of the book—perhaps due to difficulties the author encountered in getting the book approved by the censors or perhaps to invite speculation that Kant was the author of the book, thereby increasing sales. And indeed, there was widespread belief, upon the book's initial publication, that Kant had written it. The true author, however, was the young Johann Gottlieb Fichte (1762–1814). In this book, Fichte attempted to determine the compatibility between Kant's critical philosophy and the concept of divine revelation. He composed it over the course of several weeks in Königsberg in order to impress Kant and win his support. Kant was indeed impressed. The cash-strapped Fichte had asked Kant for a loan, and rather than give him money, Kant arranged for Fichte to sell his manuscript to Kant's publisher. A positive review of the book in the *Allgemeine Literatur Zeitung* claimed that Kant must be the author of the work, prompting Kant to publish a letter in the following month's edition giving credit and honor to Fichte. Fichte was, thus, launched from obscurity and became a significant philosophical figure (Wood 2010a, viii–ix).

Fichte's *Attempt at a Critique of All Revelation*, while similar to Kant's, differs in some important respects. Fichte follows Kant in grounding religion in morality rather than theoretical cognition or nonrational feelings. Revelation itself cannot be grounded on theoretical knowledge, and in fact, all we can ever know is that it is *possible* that some supposed revelation was truly given by God—that is, so long as this supposed revelation is moral in nature. All of this is, of course, Kantian terrain, though as Allen Wood argues, religion is perhaps for Fichte more closely connected with moral motivation than it is for Kant (Wood 2010a, xvi). In any case, Kant's *Religion* does quite a bit more than simply argue that we cannot have theoretical knowledge of the existence of revelation and that morality must serve as the criterion for any possible revelation. As we have seen, the *Religion* represents an intense engagement with a specific revelation, interpreted through the lens of practical reason, and a sustained argument for the value of revelation as a (ultimately dispensable) vehicle for the promotion of pure moral religion.

The reception and influence of Kant's *Religion* specifically cannot be easily separated from the reception and influence of Kant's philosophy of religion more broadly. Walter Jaeschke has called the 1790s the "decade of the moral God" on account of the widespread influence of Kant's philosophy of religion (82). This popularity was due perhaps less to Kant's writings directly than to the popularization of them by Karl Reinhold in his *Letters on the Kantian Philosophy*, which Karl Ameriks has called "arguably the most influential work ever written concerning Kant" (ix). These *Letters* originally appeared as a series of articles in the journal *Der Teusche Merkur* in 1786–87 and were published in expanded book form in 1790. Reinhold attempted to expound and make accessible the forbidding prose of the first *Critique* and the density of Kant's critical philosophy. In doing so, Reinhold placed heavy emphasis on the *positive* side of Kant's attack on traditional philosophical theology, namely, the space that Kant's once-and-for-all destruction of the old proofs of God's existence opens for *moral faith*. The ideas that formed the background to the *Religion*, ideas we discussed in Chapter 1 and encountered in Kant's first edition Preface, found a large audience thanks to Reinhold.

It would not be long, however, before serious doubts were raised about Kant's ethicotheology. Jaeschke organizes the critique of Kant's ethicotheology in the late 1790s into three basic objections. Before looking at these objections, it will be helpful to remember that for Kant belief in God is first and foremost a response to the disjunction between happiness and virtue in the world. Of course, as rational beings, happiness should never be a motive for moral action, and Kant insists upon our ability to act morally without any other incentive than respect for the moral law itself. In this respect, morality has no need of God, and the atheist should be just as capable of moral action as the theist. And yet, Kant also insists that human beings always act with reference to some end; without an end in view, how could we ever be determined to act at all? And as sensible beings that experience natural inclinations, we unavoidably make happiness (the satisfaction of inclinations) our end. We do make this end morally acceptable, of course, by aiming not at happiness at any cost but by setting the highest good as our ultimate end—happiness proportioned to virtue. But since happiness and virtue are not causally linked—happiness does not directly produce virtuous action, nor does virtuous action necessarily lead to happiness—we must postulate God's existence in order for the highest good to be possible. So, it seems that when we consider ourselves simply as rational beings, the atheist is on at least equal footing with the theist in his ability to act morally; yet, with respect to the final end, the atheist has cause for despair, and indeed may find his adherence to his moral vocation weakened on account of the seeming impossibility of attaining the final end that he has set for himself, as Kant says in the third *Critique* (5:452–53).

With this in mind, let us consider the common objections to Kant's ethicotheology. The first objection is that even if practical reason were to fall into self-contradiction without the postulation of God's existence—that is, if practical reason were to set as its end something ultimately unattainable without God—this in itself is not a proof of God's existence. Of course, this objection loses some of its force when we bear in mind that Kant does not pretend to have provided a definitive proof of God's existence; God is, for Kant, the object of a moral *faith*. But even with this in mind, the objection is a significant one. Can we really be justified in believing in the existence of God simply because we have a human need for it? What ultimately distinguishes Kant's moral argument from mere wishful thinking? It is not clear that Kant can provide an answer. This leads to the second objection to Kant's ethicotheology, that practical reason does not, in fact, fall into self-contradiction without the presupposition of God, because one is not exempt from doing what the moral law requires if the highest good turns out to be unattainable; and if we are truly free, as Kant insists, then we *can* do what the moral law requires even if we do not believe that happiness will result. So, there is no contradiction here, and the justification for postulating God's existence disappears. Third, it may be the case that the idea of God actually *hinders* morality or perhaps makes morality impossible altogether. For, how would it be possible for one who truly believes that God will mete out happiness in proportion to virtue to act purely out of respect for the moral law? A moral faith in God might very well be detrimental to morality (Jaeschke, 87).

Dissatisfaction with Kant's philosophy of religion was not simply related to problems inherent in the ethicotheology. Kant's systematic interpretation of the content of Christian revelation in terms of morality could be seen as reductive, or at least one dimensional, and as a failure to take true measure of the spirit and perhaps even the philosophical significance of historical revelation. The young Hegel took quite seriously Kant's attempt to interpret positive, historical religion in light of reason, as can be seen in an early unpublished essay, "The Positivity of the Christian Religion." His early adherence there to Kant's ethicotheology is unmistakable:

> I remark here that the general principle to be laid down as a foundation for all judgments on the varying modifications, forms, and spirit of the Christian religion is this—that the aim and essence of all true religion, our religion included, is human morality, and that all the more detailed doctrines of Christianity, all the means of propagating them, and all its obligations (whether obligations to believe or obligations to perform actions in themselves otherwise arbitrary) have their worth and their sanctity appraised according to their close or distant connection with that aim. (68)

Hegel wrote these words in 1795–96; by 1798–99, in another unpublished essay, "The Spirit of Christianity and Its Fate," he is already moving well beyond Kant's ethicotheology. While a thorough examination of these texts is not possible here, it will be instructive to look at how Hegel situates Kantian ethics in relation to Judaism in these two essays. In the earlier essay, Hegel depicts the Jews as burdened under the weight of statutory commands and living in slavish obedience to those laws, just as Kant does; and again like Kant, Hegel saw the moral teachings of Jesus as standing in opposition to Judaism. In "The Spirit of Christianity and Its Fate," however, Hegel continues to see Judaism as a slavish obedience to the law, but he comes to see Kantian ethics as involving a similar sort of slavish obedience.

And in a biting reworking of a passage from Part IV of the *Religion* that we quoted earlier (6:176), Hegel writes:

> Between the Shaman of the Tungus, the European prelate who rules church and state, the [Wogulites], and the Puritans, on the one hand, and the man who listens to his own command of duty, on the other, the difference is not that the former make themselves slaves, while the latter is free, but that the former have their lord outside themselves, while the latter carries his lord in himself, yet at the same time is his own slave. (211)

Kant's point, of course, was that while nonmoral forms of divine service may differ in style, they are one and the same in principle. Hegel's point is that as long as one feels oneself bound by a law, it does not matter whether that law is imposed from outside or one imposes it upon oneself; one is a slave to it either way. Kantian ethics is a form of servitude, on Hegel's reading, because the command of duty presupposes a disjunction between reason and inclination (212); as Kant says in his ethical writings, we experience the moral law as an unconditional command or "categorical imperative" precisely because we experience inclinations that run counter to the moral law. Thus, Kantian ethics itself is a form of slavishness and subjection, and much closer to the spirit of Judaism than Kant would have cared to admit. To this Judeo-Kantianism Hegel opposes the teaching of Jesus, which is given quintessential expression, for Hegel as for Kant, in the Sermon on the Mount. But here, unlike in the earlier "The Positivity of the Christian Religion," Jesus' sermon is not the declamation of Kantian ethics but an annulment and a fulfillment of Judeo-Kantian law. For Hegel, Kant profoundly misunderstood Jesus when he interpreted Jesus' words "love God above all else and love everyone as yourself" as a summation of the command to do one's duty out of respect for the moral law alone (see 6:160–61). Kant's interpretation "falls to the ground by its own weight, because in love all thought of duty vanishes" (213). In other words, in acting through love, one no longer experiences the law in the form of duty, as something that fights against the inclinations; reason and inclination, which Kant always opposes, find reconciliation in Jesus' teachings.

While "The Spirit of Christianity and Its Fate" represents an early stage of Hegel's attempt to overcome Kant's philosophy of religion, it is a good example of a tendency that characterizes Romanticism and Idealism in the nineteenth century more broadly: the attempt to overcome and resolve the various bifurcations and cleavages bequeathed by Kantian thought, between, for example, intuition and concept, freedom and nature, or practical and theoretical reason. Insofar as Kant's philosophy of religion itself is grounded in these dualisms, it too was something to be overcome.

Kant's philosophy of religion finds, on the whole, a much more welcome reception in the twentieth century, beginning with the work of the great Marburg Neo-Kantian Hermann Cohen. His *Religion of Reason out of the Sources of Judaism* was published not long after his death in 1919 and is widely regarded as one of the greatest works of Jewish philosophy in the nineteenth or twentieth centuries. As the title of this work indicates, Cohen does not share Kant's view of Judaism as a merely statutory religion, falling outside the scope of rational religion. On the contrary, in the Introduction to *Religion of Reason*, Cohen writes: "I do not assert that Judaism alone is the religion of reason. I try to understand how other monotheistic religions also have their fruitful share in the religion of reason, although in regard to *primary origin* this share cannot be compared with that of Judaism" (34). And like Kant's engagement with Christian revelation in the *Religion*, Cohen's claim is borne out through an extensive examination of Jewish biblical and rabbinic texts.

Kant's writings, and especially the *Religion*, were particularly important for French philosopher Paul Ricoeur. Ricoeur sees Kant's *Religion* as fitting within his own project of hermeneutic anthropology. In "A Philosophical Hermeneutics of Religion: Kant," Ricoeur writes:

> That our actual will is a bound will is the enigma that sets in motion Kant's philosophical reflection on religion. . . . It is a question of an existential historicity, for which there is no experience that is not mediated by narratives, symbols, and myths, all of which are also historical in the cultural sense of the term, as are the specific structures of any religion. All interpretation here has to take place within the limits of reason alone, yet the historical condition of captive freedom, which is the very fact of evil, finds its proper place outside of the circle of the competence of transcendental philosophy, hence of critical philosophy. (76)

In other words, what Kant examines in the *Religion* is not the *Wille* as the rational structure of the will that is determined directly by the moral law, but the power of choice (*Willkür*) that must choose between the obedience to the moral law and the empirical desire that goes hand in hand with human finitude. Man as a finite, sensible being is a *historical* being whose experience of the world is mediated by religious symbols, symbols that can promote or retard his progress in overcoming his weak and fallible nature.

Like Kant, Ricoeur was opposed to the doctrine of original sin, and for much the same reason; according to Ricoeur, original sin is a kind of conceptual monstrosity that illicitly joins the juridical category of guilt with the biological category of inheritance. And yet, this "false concept" of original sin is not to be written off altogether, because its very conceptual incoherence points to something fundamental in the avowal or confession of sin: namely, that we both originate evil and find it somehow *always already there*. Kant's doctrine of radical evil, according to Ricoeur, gives expression to this paradox. In Ricoeur's extensive engagement with evil in *The Symbolism of Evil* and in the various essays collected in *The Conflict of Interpretations*, Kant, therefore, serves as a crucial point of reference.

Kant's *Religion* also plays a significant role in the writings of Jacques Derrida, above all, in Derrida's most important text on religion, "Faith and Knowledge: The Two Sources of 'Religion' at the Limits of Reason Alone." In this text, originally presented at a seminar in Capri in 1994, Derrida asks: "*What of this 'Kantian' gesture today? What would a book be like today which, like Kant's, is entitled,* Religion within the Limits of Reason Alone?" Derrida says that the task of those gathered in Capri consists in nothing less than the

> *attempt to transpose, here and now, the circumspect and suspensive attitude, a certain* epoché *that consists—rightly or wrongly, for the issue is serious—in thinking religion or making it appear "within the limits of reason alone."* (8, italics in the original)

Derrida's reading of Kant's *Religion*—which focuses particularly on the place of the "parerga" in relation to "religion within the boundaries of mere reason"—attempts to show the instability of the borders that Kant attempts to erect between moral and statutory religion.

Moreover, Derrida is suspicious of Kant's claim that Christianity is the sole moral religion. And yet, Derrida ultimately affirms the basic Enlightenment impulse, casting his lot with what he calls

> *an unreserved taste, if not an unconditional preference, for what, in politics, is called republican democracy as a universalizable model, binding philosophy to the public "cause," to the* res publica, *to "public-ness," once again to the light of day, once again to the "lights" of the Enlightenment* <aux Lumières>, *once again to the enlightened virtue of public space, emancipating it from all external power (non-lay, non-secular), for example from religious dogmatism, orthodoxy or authority (that is, from a certain rule of the* doxa *or of belief, which, however, does not mean from all faith).* (8)

For Derrida, then, fidelity to the Enlightenment goes hand in hand with a critical interrogation of the foundational gestures of the Enlightenment. And it may well be that any positive use of Kant's thought today must proceed by way of such critical interrogation. The *Religion* is an impassioned plea for tolerance and freedom of conscience, values that we continue to affirm. And yet, the *Religion* remains a profoundly *Christian* document; Christianity is the sole moral religion, for Kant, and therefore the only vehicle suited for fulfilling the duty of humanity to bring about an ethical community. Is such a view relevant in an age in which religious conflict is not merely an inter-Christian problem? And is it adequate to deal with twenty-first-century problems of fanaticism and intolerance, problems that are in many ways a direct response to Western Enlightenment ideals found in texts like the *Religion*? These are questions that Kant leaves for us; the *Religion* is not a mere artifact of a past era but a challenge to the present that demands our continued reflection.

CHAPTER FIVE

Guide for further reading

Context

Brief treatments of Kant's life abound in the various introductions to his philosophy; for a concise overview of his life and for a comprehensive introductory treatment of his philosophy as a whole, see Guyer (2006). A great introduction for students who are new to Kant's ethics is Uleman (2010). The standard biography of Kant in English is Kuehn (2001), of which chapter 8, "Problems with Religion and Politics (1788–1795)," is especially helpful for understanding the circumstances surrounding the publication of Kant's *Religion*. Briefer accounts of these circumstances include Wood (1996) and Greene (1960). The literature on religion in the Enlightenment is vast, though good general treatments with which to begin are Byrne (1996), Cassirer (1951), and Gay (1966). For a general introduction to Christian theological issues, McGrath (2011) is a good place to start. Lohse (1999) provides a systematic survey of Luther's theology specifically. Many scholars, though not all, emphasize the influence of Kant's Pietist education on his religious thought. For an introduction to German Pietism, see Shantz and Erb (2013).

Students interested in exploring Kant's other writings on religion can do no better than to read Kant himself. His critique of the traditional proofs of God's existence can be found in both his precritical and critical writings. Kant rejected the ontological argument for God's existence in his *New Elucidation of the First Principles of Metaphysical Cognition* (1755) and the *Only Possible Basis for a Proof of the Existence of*

God (1763)—both available in the *Theoretical Philosophy 1755–1770* volume of the Cambridge Edition of the Works of Immanuel Kant. His full critique of traditional philosophical theology, however, is found in "The Ideal of Pure Reason" in the first *Critique*. Kant's ethicotheology is first articulated in the "Canon of Pure Reason" in the first *Critique*, though his ethicotheology would evolve significantly over subsequent publications. His famous statement of God, freedom, and immortality as "postulates of practical reason" is found in the "Dialectic of Pure Practical Reason" in the second *Critique*. Kant provides yet another statement of his ethicotheology in the third *Critique* (§86–§91). He also wrote several important essays on religion, including "What Does It Mean to Orient Oneself in Thinking?" (1786), "On the Miscarriage of All Philosophical Trials in Theodicy" (1791), and "The End of All Things" (1794). These three essays, along with *The Conflict of the Faculties* and the *Lectures on the Philosophical Doctrine of Religion*, can be found in the *Religion and Rational Theology* volume of The Cambridge Edition of the Works of Immanuel Kant. Wood (1970) and Wood (1978) are classic treatments of Kant's philosophy of religion. Förster (2000) provides a helpful account of the development of Kant's ethicotheology from the first *Critique* through the last unpublished writings.

Reading the text

General works on the *Religion*:

As I was writing this book, two commentaries or guides to Kant's *Religion* appeared—DiCenso (2012) and Pasternack (2014)—and one collection of essays dedicated to the *Religion* was set to appear, Michalson (2014). Rossi and Wreen (1991) is an important earlier collection of essays. Students who read German may also wish to consult Bohatec (1966), which investigates the sources that Kant used in the *Religion*, as well as the essays collected in Höffe (2010).

Works on specific issues in the *Religion*:

Part I of Kant's *Religion* has certainly drawn the most scholarly attention, both because of the intrinsic interest of evil generally and because of the contribution that Part I makes to Kant's ethical theory specifically. Recommended works include Bernstein (2002),

Michalson (1990), and Anderson-Gold and Muchnik (2010), a recent collection of essays dedicated to Kant's theory of evil. Quinn (1984, 1988) treats Kant's theory in connection with the doctrine of original sin. Two specific issues that have received scholarly attention are Kant's "missing" proof of the radical evil in human nature and the social origin of radical evil. On the first issue, see Allison (1990), Morgan (2005), Sussman (2005), and Muchnik (2010). On the second, see Wood (2010b) and Grenberg (2010).

Readers of Part II of the *Religion* will profit from the thorough examination of the concept of *Urbild* in Kant's corpus in DiCenso (2013) as well as from the discussion of his views concerning moral examples in Guyer (2011). Kant's views concerning grace and atonement in Part II and the related "remarkable antinomy" of Part III have been the subject of much study. Important essays that deal with these issues include Quinn (1986), Quinn (1990), Wolterstorff (1991), and Mariña (1997). Despland (1973) provides a detailed discussion of the *Religion* in connection with Kant's philosophy of history. Nirenberg (2013) discusses Kant's views concerning Judaism within the larger trajectory of western anti-Judaism.

Reception and influence

Jaeschke (1990) is an extremely valuable text for both the reception of Kant's philosophy of religion by his contemporaries and an understanding of Hegel's thought as a response to Kant's philosophy of religion. Beiser (1993) and di Giovanni (2005) also provide insight into the early reception of Kant, though they are not exclusively focused on his philosophy of religion. Karl Barth's classic *Protestant Theology in the Nineteenth Century* devotes a long chapter to Kant and traces his influence on subsequent generations of theologians. Kluback (1984) and Bonaunet (2004) provide extensive treatments of Hermann Cohen's philosophy of religion. Miller (2014) analyzes the influence of Kant on the thought of Jacques Derrida, with a particular focus on the philosophy of religion.

BIBLIOGRAPHY

Allison, Henry E. (1990). *Kant's Theory of Freedom*. New York: Cambridge University Press.
Anderson-Gold, Sharon. (2001). *Unnecessary Evil: History and Moral Progress in the Philosophy of Immanuel Kant*. Albany: State University of New York Press.
Anderson-Gold, Sharon and Pablo Muchnik, eds. (2010). *Kant's Anatomy of Evil*. New York: Cambridge University Press.
Barth, Karl. (1973). *Protestant Theology in the Nineteenth Century: Its Background & History*. Valley Forge: Judson Press.
Beiser, Frederick C. (1993). *The Fate of Reason: German Philosophy from Kant to Fichte*. Cambridge, MA: Harvard University Press.
Bernstein, Richard J. (2002). *Radical Evil: A Philosophical Interrogation*. Malden, MA: Polity Press.
Bohatec, Josef. (1966). *Die Religionsphilosophie Kants in der "Religion innerhalb der Grenzen der blossen Vernunft": mit besonderer Berücksichtigung ihrer theologisch-dogmatischen Quellen*. Hildesheim: Olms.
Bonaunet, Ketil. (2004). *Hermann Cohen's Kantian Philosophy of Religion*. New York: Peter Lang.
Byrne, James. (1996). *Glory, Jest, and Riddle: Religious Thought in the Enlightenment*. London: SCM Press.
Cassirer, Ernst. (1951). *The Philosophy of the Enlightenment*. Princeton: Princeton University Press.
Cohen, Hermann. (1972). *Religion of Reason out of the Sources of Judaism*. Translated by Simon Kaplan. New York: Frederick Ungar.
Derrida, Jacques. (1998). "Faith and Knowledge: The Two Sources of 'Religion' at the Limits of Reason Alone." In *Religion*. Edited by Jacques Derrida and Gianni Vattimo. Translated by Samuel Weber. Stanford: Stanford University Press. 1–78.
Despland, Michel. (1973). *Kant on History and Religion*. Montreal: McGill-Queen's University Press.
DiCenso, James J. (2011). *Kant, Religion, and Politics*. New York: Cambridge University Press.

—. (2012). *Kant's Religion within the Boundaries of Mere Reason: A Commentary*. New York: Cambridge University Press.
—. (2013). "The Concept of Urbild in Kant's Philosophy of Religion." *Kant-Studien* 104: 100–32.
di Giovanni, George. (2005). *Freedom and Religion in Kant and His Immediate Successors: The Vocation of Humankind, 1774–1800*. New York: Cambridge University Press.
Fackenheim, Emil L. (1996). *The God Within: Kant, Schelling, and Historicity*. Edited by John Burbidge. Toronto: University of Toronto Press.
Fenves, Peter. (2003). *Late Kant: Towards Another Law of the Earth*. New York: Routledge.
Fichte, Johann G. (2010). *Attempt at a Critique of All Revelation*. Edited by Allen Wood. Translated by Garrett Green. New York: Cambridge University Press.
Firestone, Chris L. and Stephen R. Palmquist. (2006). *Kant and the New Philosophy of Religion*. Bloomington: Indiana University Press.
Firestone, Chris L. and Nathan Jacobs. (2008). *In Defense of Kant's Religion*. Bloomington & Indianapolis: Indiana University Press.
Förster, Eckart. (2000). *Kant's Final Synthesis: An Essay on the Opus postumum*. Cambridge, MA: Harvard University Press.
Gay, Peter. (1966). *The Enlightenment: The Rise of Modern Paganism*. New York: Norton.
Greene, Theodore M. (1960). "The Historical Context and Religious Significance of Kant's Religion." In *Religion within the Limits of Reason Alone*. Edited by Immanuel Kant. Translated by Theodore M. Greene and Hoyt H. Hudson. New York: Harper & Row. ix–lxxviii.
Grenberg, Jeanine M. (2010). "Social Dimensions of Kant's Conception of Radical Evil." In *Kant's Anatomy of Evil*. Edited by Sharon Anderson-Gold and Pablo Muchnik. New York: Cambridge University Press.
Guyer, Paul. (2006). *Kant*. New York: Routledge.
—. (2011). "Examples of Moral Possibility." In *Kant and Education: Interpretations and Commentary*. Edited by Klas Roth and Chris W. Surprenant. New York: Routledge. 124–38.
Habermas, Jürgen, ed. (2008). "The Boundary Between Faith and Knowledge: On the Reception and Contemporary Importance of Kant's Philosophy of Religion." In *Between Naturalism and Religion: Philosophical Essays*. Malden, MA: Polity Press. 209–47.
Hegel, Georg W. F. (1971). *Early Theological Writings*. Translated by T. M. Knox. Philadelphia: University of Pennsylvania Press.
Höffe, Otfried, ed. (2010). *Die Religion innerhalb der Grenzen der bloßen Vernunft*. Berlin: Akademie Verlag.

Hume, David. (1992). "The Natural History of Religion." In *Writings on Religion*. Edited by Antony Flew. Chicago: Open Court. 107–82.
Jaeschke, Walter. (1990). *Reason in Religion: The Foundations of Hegel's Philosophy of Religion*. Translated by J. Michael Stewart and Peter C. Hodgson. Berkeley: University of California Press.
Kant, Immanuel. (1991). "Idea for a Universal History with a Cosmopolitan Purpose." In *Political Writings*. Edited by H. S. Reiss. Translated by H. B. Nisbet. New York: Cambridge University Press. 41–53.
—. (1992). *Theoretical Philosophy 1755–1770*. Edited and Translated by David Walford in collaboration with Ralf Meerbote. New York: Cambridge University Press.
—. (1996a). *Groundwork of the Metaphysics of Morals*. In *Practical Philosophy*. Edited and Translated by Mary J. Gregor. New York: Cambridge University Press.
—. (1996b). *Lectures on Philosophical Theology*. In *Religion and Rational Theology*. Edited by Allen W. Wood and George di Giovanni. Translated by Allen W. Wood. New York: Cambridge University Press.
—. (1996c). *Metaphysics of Morals*. In *Practical Philosophy*. Edited and Translated by Mary J. Gregor. New York: Cambridge University Press.
—. (1996d). "On the Miscarriage of All Philosophical Trials in Theodicy." In *Religion and Rational Theology*. Edited by Allen W. Wood and George di Giovanni. Translated by George di Giovanni. New York: Cambridge University Press.
—. (1996e). *Religion within the Boundaries of Mere Reason*. In *Religion and Rational Theology*. Edited by Allen W. Wood and George di Giovanni. Translated by George di Giovanni. New York: Cambridge University Press.
—. (1996f). *Critique of Practical Reason*. In *Practical Philosophy*. Edited and Translated by Mary J. Gregor. New York: Cambridge University Press.
—. (1998). *Critique of Pure Reason*. Edited and Translated by Paul Guyer and Allen Wood. New York: Cambridge University Press.
—. (2000). *Critique of the Power of Judgment*. Edited by Paul Guyer. Translated by Paul Guyer and Eric Matthews. New York: Cambridge University Press.
Kluback, William. (1984). *Hermann Cohen: The Challenge of a Religion of Reason*. Chico, CA: Scholars Press.
Kuehn, Manfred. (2001). *Kant: A Biography*. New York: Cambridge University Press.
Lohse, Bernhard. (1999). *Martin Luther's Theology: Its Historic and Systematic Development*. Minneapolis: Augsburg Fortress Press.

Mariña, Jacqueline. (1997). "Kant on Grace: A Reply to His Critics." *Religious Studies* 33: 379–400.
McGrath, Alister E. (2011). *Christian Theology: An Introduction.* 5th edition. Malden, MA: Wiley-Blackwell.
Michalson, Gordon. (1990). *Fallen Freedom: Kant on Radical Evil and Moral Regeneration.* New York: Cambridge University Press.
—. ed. (2014). *Kant's Religion within the Boundaries of Mere Reason: A Critical Guide.* New York: Cambridge University Press.
Miller, Eddis N. (2014). *Kantian Transpositions: Derrida and the Philosophy of Religion.* Evanston: Northwestern University Press.
Morgan, Seriol. (2005). "The Missing Formal Proof of Humanity's Radical Evil in Kant's *Religion*." *Philosophical Review* 114: 63–114.
Muchnik, Pablo. (2009). *Kant's Theory of Evil: An Essay on the Dangers of Self-Love and the Aprioricity of History.* Lanham, MD: Lexington Books.
—. (2010). "An Alternative Proof of the Universal Propensity to Evil." In *Kant's Anatomy of Evil.* Edited by Sharon Anderson-Gold and Pablo Muchnik. New York: Cambridge University Press.
Nirenberg, David. (2013). *Anti-Judaism: The Western Tradition.* New York: Norton.
Pasternak, Lawrence. (2014). *A Routledge Philosophy Guidebook to Kant on Religion within the Boundaries of Mere Reason.* New York: Routledge.
Quinn, Philip L. (1984). "Original Sin, Radical Evil and Moral Identity." *Faith and Philosophy* 1(2): 188–202.
—. (1986). "Christian Atonement and Kantian Justification." *Faith and Philosophy* 3(4): 440–62.
—. (1988). "In Adam's Fall, We Sinned All." *Philosophical Topics* 16(2): 89–118.
—. (1990). "Saving Faith from Kant's Remarkable Antinomy." *Faith and Philosophy* 7(4): 418–33.
Reinhold, Karl L. (2005). *Letters on the Kantian Philosophy.* Edited by Karl Ameriks. Translated by James Hebbeler. New York: Cambridge University Press.
Ricoeur, Paul. (1974). *The Conflict of Interpretations.* Edited by Don Ihde. Evanston: Northwestern University Press.
—. (1995). "A Philosophical Hermeneutics of Religion: Kant." *Figuring the Sacred: Religion, Narrative, and Imagination.* Edited by Mark I. Wallace. Translated by David Pellauer. Minneapolis: Fortress Press. 75–92.
—. (1967). *The Symbolism of Evil.* Translated by Emerson Buchanan. Boston: Beacon Press.
Rossi, Philip J. and Michael Wreen, eds. (1991). *Kant's Philosophy of Religion Reconsidered.* Bloomington and Indianapolis: Indiana University Press.

Shantz, Douglas H. and Peter C. Erb. (2013). *An Introduction to German Pietism: Protestant Renewal at the Dawn of Modern Europe*. Baltimore: Johns Hopkins University Press.

Silber, John R. (1960). "The Ethical Significance of Kant's Religion." In *Religion within the Limits of Reason Alone*. Translated by Theodore M. Greene and Hoyt H. Hudson, lxxix–cxxxiv. New York: Harper & Row.

Stanglin, Keith D. (2007). *Arminius on the Assurance of Salvation: The Context, Roots, and Shape of the Leiden Debate, 1603–1609*. Leiden: Brill.

Sussman, David. (2005). "Perversity of the Heart." *Philosophical Review* 114: 153–77.

Uleman, Jennifer K. (2010). *An Introduction to Kant's Moral Philosophy*. New York: Cambridge University Press.

Wolterstorff, Nicholas. (1991). "Conundrum's in Kant's Rational Religion." In *Kant's Philosophy of Religion Reconsidered*. Edited by Philip J. Rossi and Michael Wreen. Bloomington, IN: Indiana University Press.

Wood, Allen. (1970). *Kant's Moral Religion*. Ithaca: Cornell University Press.

—. (1978). *Kant's Rational Theology*. Ithaca: Cornell University Press.

—. (1996). "General Introduction." In *Religion and Rational Theology*. Edited by Immanuel Kant. New York: Cambridge University Press.

—. (2010a). "Introduction." In *Attempt at a Critique of All Revelation*. Johann G. Fichte. Translated by Garrett Green, vii–xxvii. New York: Cambridge University Press.

—. (2010b). "Kant and the Intelligibility of Evil." In *Kant's Anatomy of Evil*. Edited by Sharon Anderson-Gold and Pablo Muchnik. New York: Cambridge University Press.

INDEX

Abraham   83, 84, 126
Adam   20, 48, 49, 52, 81
akedah   83
*Allgemeine Literatur
    Zeitung*   133
Ameriks, Karl   134
angelic miracles   83, 84
    see also individual entries
animality   25–6
    see also predisposition, to
    animality
anthropological research   40, 47
apostle   36, 63, 113
assertoric faith *see* faith
atonement   10, 11, 19, 75–6, 77,
    143
*Attempt at a Critique of All
    Revelation*   133

baptism   131
Barth, Karl   143
belief *see* faith
Berlin censors   6
Berlinische Monatsschrift   5, 54
Bible   2, 63, 69, 95
Biester, Johann Erich   5, 6
bin Laden, Osama   31
blind faith *see* faith
Book of Revelation   109

call, mystery of   112
"Canon of Pure Reason"   142
Capri   139

categorical command, of moral
    law   13, 51, 52, 70, 137
    see also unconditional
    command, of moral law
Catholic Church   64
Catholicism *see* Catholic Church
Catholics   1
causality, principle of   112
Christian Church   20, 92
Christian doctrine   21, 47, 57, 81
    of grace and atonement   10,
    11, 59
    of original sin   19, 20, 39, 53,
    60
    of Trinity   110
    see also doctrine of original sin
Christian dogma *see* dogma(s)
Christian faith *see* faith
Christianity   9, 11, 19, 80, 82, 95,
    96, 97, 106, 107, 111,
    114, 117, 119, 120, 136,
    137, 140
Christian revelation   9, 17, 111,
    136, 138
Christian scriptures   9, 19, 103,
    120
    see also Jewish scriptures;
    scripture(s)
Christian theology   19, 36, 53, 64,
    66, 109, 110
Christian tradition *see* tradition(s)
"Christology" *see* Christian
    theology

church   11, 90–2
    historical   11, 99
    invisible (*see* invisible church)
    true visible (*see* true visible church)
    universal history   107
    visible (*see* visible church)
    see also individual entries
church-going, purpose of   130–1
"church invisible" *vs.* "church visible"   90–1
clergy   2
Cohen, Hermann   138, 143
commands, of moral law *see* moral law(s)
communion   131–2
conditional command, of moral law   13
    see also moral law(s)
Conflict of Interpretations, The   139
Conflict of the Faculties, The   7, 18, 48, 142
"congregation"   91, 109, 119, 120
conscience   3, 12, 27, 45, 48, 60, 108, 109, 120, 123, 125–7, 130, 140
corruption   32, 33, 55, 74, 85, 86, 113
counterfeit service   12, 114–32
    of God, in statutory religion   120–7
critical philosophy, and divine revelation   133
Critique of Practical Reason   5
Critique of Pure Reason   3, 5
Critique of the Power of Judgment   5
culture, development of   26, 62

"decade of the moral God"   134
"deed"   43
delusion(s)
    definition   120–1

practical   121
religious   12, 60, 114, 120, 121, 122, 123, 125, 129, 131
demonic miracles   83, 84, 126–7
    see also individual entries
depravity   45–8
Derrida, Jacques   139, 140, 143
Der Teusche Merkur   134
diabolical evil   31–2
    see also evil
"Dialectic of Pure Practical Reason"   142
DiCenso, James   60
direct revelation *see* revelation
disposition *(Gesinnung)*   30
"divine origin"   62, 68, 98
divine punishment *see* punishment
divine revelation   97, 98, 108, 116
    and critical philosophy   133
    see also revelation
doctrine of original sin   9, 10, 19, 20, 21, 37, 39, 43, 48, 57, 139, 143
    see also Christian doctrine, of original sin
doctrine of radical evil *see* radical evil
"Doctrine of Right"   89
dogma(s)   2, 3, 4, 9, 12, 18, 19, 21, 48, 66, 68, 94, 99, 109, 117
dogmatic faith *see* faith

Easter Book Fair (Leipzig)   6
ecclesiastical faith   11, 92–106, 108, 117, 124
    see also faith
ecclesiastical service   124
election, mystery of   112–14
"End of All Things, The"   142
English and Scottish Enlightenment   1
"enlightened absolutism"   5

Enlightenment   1, 2, 5, 19, 20, 108, 125, 140
enthusiasm *(Schwärmerei)*   55, 59, 60, 74, 91, 132
epistemology, of salvation *see* salvation
erudition   116, 117
ethical community   11, 86, 87–91, 94, 95, 107, 114, 130, 140
ethical laws, people of God under   88–90
"Ethical Significance of Kant's *Religion,* The"   30
ethicotheology   3, 16, 134, 142
    common objections to   135–6
Europe   1
Eve   20, 48, 49, 53, 81
evil   10, 11, 27, 28, 32, 38
    characteristic of mankind, as species   36–53
    definition   29–30
    disposition   30, 31, 36, 39, 47, 48, 51, 73, 75, 76
    innate   37
    judgment about being evil   33–6
    nature   37
    propensity to   37, 40, 41–4, 45, 46, 47, 51, 52, 85
    and radically evil   22–33
    universal   48
    see also individual entries
evil principle's rightful claim, to dominion over human being   80–1
    see also good principle's rightful claim, to dominion over human being
existence of God *see* God

faith   3, 12
    assertoric   115
    blind   4

Christian   11
dogmatic   56
ecclesiastical (*see* ecclesiastical faith)
historical (*see* historical faith)
moral (*see* moral faith)
pure rational   100
rational   15, 18, 104, 106
    in rationality   20
reflective   56, 59
and religion   96
"saving faith" (*see* "saving faith")
"slavish faith" (*see* "slavish faith")
supernatural   4
"Faith and Knowledge: The Two Sources of 'Religion' at the Limits of Reason Alone"   139
Fall of Adam and Eve   48, 80
    see also individual entries
fanaticism   60, 140
Fenves, Peter   33
fetishism   12, 93, 114, 120, 123, 124–5, 129
Fichte, Johann Gottlieb   133
formal *vs.* material aspects of religion   16–17
frailty   44
Frederick II (the Great)   5
Frederick William II   5, 18
freedom   10, 18, 24, 32, 33, 37, 40, 42, 43, 46, 48–51, 62, 72, 81, 84, 87, 89, 91, 98, 102, 103, 108–13, 138, 142
    of conscience   3, 12, 140
    human   21, 38, 50, 112, 128
    of thought   2, 5, 60, 109
free will   11, 29, 40, 49, 62
French *Lumières*   1

Garden of Eden 20
"General Remark" 54–60, 79, 81–4, 109–11, 127–9
Genesis 2-3, Kant's reading of 48–53
German *Aufklärung* 1
Germany 5, 106
God
  belief in 134
  benevolent ruler 111
  commands 20
  counterfeit service 120–7
  existence 2, 3, 15, 16, 17, 134, 135, 136, 141
  grace 10, 57, 77, 113, 128, 131, 132
  holiness 131
  as holy lawgiver 111
  holy will 70, 71
  idea 13, 15, 16, 55, 56, 65, 76, 93, 110, 111, 116, 136
  just judge 111
  mercy 131
  moral faith (*see* moral faith)
  nature 3
  pleasing to 11
  prohibition 52
  supernatural being 11
Goethe, Johann Wolfgang von 20
good
  being 27, 28
  conduct, result of 15
  disposition 30, 31, 39
  predispositions to 42
good principle's rightful claim, to dominion over human being 63
  difficulties in reality and their solution 69–79
  objective reality 67–9
  personified idea, of good principle 63–6
  see also evil principle's rightful claim, to dominion over human being
good principle's victory, and founding of kingdom of God on earth 84–6
  historical representation 105–9
  philosophical representation 86–105
"good will" 56
Gospel of John 64, 65
Gospel of Matthew 119
grace 10, 54–7, 59–60, 77–9, 90, 102, 113, 124, 128, 129, 131, 132, 143
  see also "means of grace"
Greek moral teachings 81
  see also moral teachings
Groundwork for the Metaphysics of Morals 5, 67, 68, 70

happiness 14, 15, 26, 27, 56, 65, 73, 76, 89, 99, 119, 135, 136
  moral *vs.* physical 72
  moral worthiness 4
  and virtue 134
Hegel, Georg Wilhelm Friedrich 136, 137
Herder, Johann Gottfried von 20
hermeneutic principles 7, 47, 48
"highest good" 4, 15, 56, 88, 93, 109, 135
historical being 65, 139
historical church *see* church
historical faith 12, 18, 82, 95, 96, 99, 100, 103, 104, 107, 114, 124, 125, 127
  see also faith
historical religion 3, 4, 5, 7, 9, 16, 17, 19, 21, 56, 68, 79, 86, 136
  see also religion

historical representation, and dominion of good principle on earth 105–9
historical revelations 9, 10, 16, 17, 93, 117, 136
Hitler, Adolf 29, 31
holiness 70–2, 108, 111, 112, 118, 131
human being(s) 9, 10, 25, 31–2, 38, 55–6, 71–2
  battle of good against evil principle 60–84
  evil and radically evil 22
    animality 25–6
    humanity 26
    personality 26–33
  evil characteristic of mankind as species 36–48
  free being 13, 15, 32, 40, 112
  Genesis 2-3, Kant's reading of 48–53
  judgment about being evil 33–6
  moral culture 124
  moral regeneration 11
  vs. nonhuman animals 14–15
  rational 4, 14, 56
  rules/practical principles 24
  sensible 4, 14, 15, 56, 70, 129, 135
  see also humanity
humanity 10, 15, 20, 26, 27, 36, 42, 47, 50, 53, 61, 62, 65, 66, 69, 87, 104, 107, 140
  contingent 41
  education 2
  moral faith 4
  in moral perfection 67
  predisposition 85
  see also human being(s); predisposition, to humanity
human knowledge, limits of 3, 64, 111, 115, 116

Hume, David 122
hypothetical command, of moral law *see* conditional command, of moral law

"*Idea for a Universal History with a Cosmopolitan Aim*" 85, 90
Idealism 138
"Ideal of Pure Reason, The" 142
illumination 55, 59
immortality 70, 71, 72, 142
impurity 44–5
inclination(s)
  definition 14
  natural 4, 14, 23, 24, 25, 27, 32, 38, 44, 46, 61, 62, 67, 70, 71, 135
  nonmoral 34
  vs. reason 137
infinite punishment *see* punishment
innate 39–40
  see also evil
"inner principle of maxims, the" 30
institutional religion *see* religion
invisible church 90–1, 94, 95
  see also church
Isaac 83, 126, 127

Jaeschke, Walter 134
Jena 6
Jesus Christ 10, 11, 19, 63, 64, 65, 66, 68, 69, 70, 75, 76, 80, 81, 82, 83, 91, 103, 114, 117, 118–19, 120, 124, 130, 136, 137
Jewish scriptures 106, 107
  see also Christian scriptures; scripture(s)
Jewish theocracy 80
  see also theocracy
Jews 107, 136

Judaism   80, 81, 82, 90, 96, 106, 107, 119, 120, 136, 137, 138, 143
judgment about being evil *see* human being(s)
juridical laws   86, 87
juridico-civil state   86
justice (divine)   76, 77, 79, 89, 113

Kantian ethics   136, 137
"Kingdom of Evil"   80
kingdom of God on earth, and good principle's victory   84–6
  historical representation   105–9
  philosophical representation   86–105
Kingdom of Heaven, arrival of   109
Königsberg   133
Kuehn, Manfred   6

laws *see individual entries*
laws of nature   32, 89, 112
learned religion   98, 114, 116, 117, 119, 120
  see also religion
Lectures on the Philosophical Doctrine of Religion   142
legality   45, 82, 87, 89
Leipzig   6
Letters on the Kantian Philosophy   134
Letter to the Romans   36
Luther, Martin   10, 77, 141
Lutheranism   5, 64

mankind, evil characteristic of   36
  Genesis 2-3, Kant's reading of   48–53
  innate   39–40
  nature   37–9
  propensity   41–4
    depravity   45–8

frailty   44
impurity   44–5
see also human being(s); humanity
material *vs.* formal aspects of religion   16–17
maxim(s)   24, 25, 28–31, 33–6, 38, 42, 43–5, 47, 52, 55, 59, 61, 67, 72, 75, 104, 108
"means of grace"   54, 56, 59, 127–8
  baptism   131
  church-going   130–1
  communion   131–2
  praying   129–30
  see also grace
mechanical self-love   25
  see also self-love
"mercenary faith" *see* "slavish faith"
"mere cult," religion of *see* religion, of rogation
Metaphysics of Morals   16, 17, 89
miracles   54, 55, 56, 59, 69, 81–4, 117, 127
  see also individual entries
moral agents   26
moral being   11, 15, 26, 66, 73, 88
moral evil   22, 26, 37, 42, 43, 49, 50, 53, 61, 62, 63, 87
  see also evil
moral faith   4, 12, 92, 96, 99, 100, 101, 102, 103, 104, 105, 106, 111, 125, 134, 135, 136
  see also faith
"moral feeling"   27
moral God   2, 4, 116, 134
moral good   22, 25, 37, 62, 63, 128, 130
moral happiness *vs.* physical happiness   72
  see also happiness

morality   2, 3, 9, 10, 18, 21, 24,
      25, 35, 37, 47, 48, 55, 56,
      57, 59, 61, 62, 64, 69, 73,
      79, 80, 83, 84, 87, 89, 91,
      92, 96, 97, 98, 110, 112,
      114, 121, 126, 127, 129,
      134, 135, 136
   independence   13
   and religion   13–15
   religion in   133
   self-subsistence   13
moral law(s)   4, 26, 40, 44, 56,
      62, 67, 71, 87, 89, 135
   adulteration   52
   as categorical imperative   13,
      51, 52, 70, 137
   conditional command   13
   demand for   29
   dignity   32
   incentive   27, 34, 45, 47
   respect for   24
   to self-love   30, 31, 43, 45,
      46, 85
   unconditional command (*see*
      unconditional command,
      of moral law)
   unconditional
      prioritization   29
   violation   28, 32, 33, 45
   see also individual entries
moral perfection   10, 11, 25,
      64–8, 70, 71, 72, 80, 81,
      91, 92, 95, 103, 129
moral propensity   42, 43
moral religion   3, 4, 5, 9, 11, 12,
      16, 17, 18, 21, 58, 64, 80,
      81, 82, 83, 92, 93, 94, 95,
      96, 97, 105, 106, 107,
      111, 113, 114, 115, 120,
      121, 128, 134, 139, 140
   see also pure moral religion;
      religion
moral rigorism   23, 29

moral teachings   66
   Christianity   82
   Greek   81
   of Jesus   119, 136
   Judaism   107
mystery(ies)   53, 54, 55, 56, 59, 61,
      109, 111
   of call   112
   definition   110
   of election   112–14
   of satisfaction   112
"Mystery of Morality" (MoM)
      thesis   61, 63, 66, 67

*Natural History of Religion,
   The*   122
natural inclinations *see*
      inclination(s)
naturalist   116
natural propensity, to evil   42
natural religion   114, 115,
      116–17, 119, 120, 123
   see also religion
nature   37–9, 40
   ethical state   86–8
   evil   37
   of God   3
   see also laws of nature
Navigator Islands   47
*New Elucidation of the First
   Principles of Metaphysical
   Cognition*   141
New Testament   69, 95, 118, 119,
      120
New Zealand   47
nonhuman animals *vs.* human
      beings   14–15
nonmoral incentive   34, 45, 52
nonmoral inclination *see*
      inclination(s)

objective reality, of moral
      perfection   67–9

"Of Effects of Grace"   54, 56, 57, 59, 60, 128
"Of the Struggle of the Good Principle with the Evil Principle for Sovereignty over Man"   6
Old Testament   95, 119, 120
Only Possible Basis for a Proof of the Existence of God   141–2
"On Radical Evil in Human Nature"   5
"On the Miscarriage of All Philosophical Trials in Theodicy"   5, 142
ontology, of salvation *see* salvation
origin
   "according to reason" *vs.* "according to time"   49, 62
   definition   49
original sin *see* doctrine of original sin

"pagan superstition"   131
   see also superstition
parerga (parergon)   54, 55, 56, 79, 81, 139
particular rule   118–19
Paul (the apostle)   36, 37, 44, 46, 63, 76, 77, 113
peccatum derivativum (derivative sin)   43
peccatum originarium (original sin)   43
Pelagius   20
people of God
   under ethical laws   88–90
   and human organization   90–2
personality   26–33
personified idea, of good principle   63–6
"perversity" of the heart   45, 46
"A Philosophical Hermeneutics of Religion: Kant"   138

philosophical representation, of good principle's victory   86
church   90–2
ecclesiastical faith   92–6
ethical community   87–8
kingdom of God   99–105
nature, ethical state of   86–7
people of God under ethical laws   88–90
pure faith of religion   96–9
physical happiness *vs.* moral happiness   72
   see also happiness
physical propensity   42
political community   87, 88, 107
political state   86–90, 94, 106, 111
"Positivity of the Christian Religion, The"   136, 137
practical delusions   121
   see also delusion(s)
praying   129–30
predisposition
   to animality   25, 26, 27, 62, 85
   to the good   10, 25, 32, 50, 53, 54, 62, 85
   to humanity   26, 27, 61, 62, 85
"priestcraft" *(Pfaffentum)*   3, 114, 123, 124–5, 131
project of Religion *see* religion
propensity, to evil   37, 40, 41–4, 51, 52, 85
   depravity   45–8
   frailty   44
   impurity   44–5
   see also evil
Protestant Reformation   1
Protestant(s)   1
   denominations   64
   doctrine of atonement   76
   reformers   77
   tradition   75

Protestant Theology in the Nineteenth Century 143
Prussia 5, 6
punishment 23–4, 76–7, 81, 87, 101, 102, 107, 108
   divine 20
   infinite 10, 75, 76
pure faith of religion 96–9
pure moral religion 11, 12, 16, 21, 114, 134
   see also moral religion
pure rationalist 116
pure rational religion 3, 11, 12, 16
   see also rational religion
pure religion of reason 3, 16

radical evil 6, 10, 31, 73, 84, 85, 86
   doctrine of 139
   in human nature 19–60, 143
   social origin 143
rational being(s) 4, 14, 15, 56, 70, 88, 89, 101, 134, 135
rational faith 15, 18, 104, 106
   see also faith
rationalists 116
rational religion 2, 3, 4, 9, 11, 12, 14, 16, 17, 19, 21, 68, 93, 98, 138
   see also pure rational religion; religion
reality, of moral perfection
   difficulties and their solution 69–79
   objective 67–9
reason
   impotence 56
   vs. inclination 137
   power 2
   and revelation 16, 17
reception and influence, of Kant's philosophy of religion 133

"reciprocal love" 85
reflective faith *see* faith
Reinhold, Karl 134
religion 5
   definition 115
   Enlightenment view 2
   and faith 96
   formal aspect 16
   of good life-conduct 58
   historical (*see* historical religion)
   by Immanuel Kant 3
   institutional 2
   learned (*see* learned religion)
   material aspect 16, 17
   monotheistic 138
   moral (*see* moral religion)
   morality 13–15, 133
   moral motivation 134
   moral principle 123
   natural (*see* natural religion)
   philosophical analysis 5
   philosophical hermeneutics 21
   philosophical treatments 1
   philosophic morals 17
   project 16–19
   rational (*see* rational religion)
   of reason 9
   revealed (*see* revealed religion)
   of rogation 58
   service of God in 114–20
   statutory (*see* statutory religion)
   universal 116
Religion and Rational Theology 142
Religion of Reason out of the Sources of Judaism 138
religious delusion 12, 60, 114, 120, 121, 122, 123, 125, 129, 131
   see also delusion(s)
religious institutions 2

revealed religion   2, 12, 17, 19, 114, 115, 116, 117, 120
    see also religion
revelation   12, 21, 95, 96
    attitudes toward   2
    Christian (see Christian revelation)
    direct   126, 127
    divine (see divine revelation)
    existence   134
    historical (see historical revelations)
    moral interpretation   18
    and reason   16, 17
    supernatural   82, 117
    value   134
Ricoeur, Paul   138, 139
rigorism see moral rigorism
Romans   44, 74, 113
Romanticism   138
Rosicrucians   5

St Augustine   20, 77
salvation   11, 57, 66, 74, 77, 78, 108, 113, 125
    epistemology   73
    ontology   73
Satan   53, 63, 66, 80, 81
satisfaction, mystery of   112
"saving faith"   99, 100, 102, 103, 104
    see also faith
scripture(s)   3, 5, 6, 7, 9, 10, 12, 19, 51, 53, 63, 64, 65, 80, 81, 82, 83, 94, 95, 105, 108, 114, 117, 121, 126, 129
    certification   97
    Christian (see Christian scriptures)
    exposition   97, 98
    Jewish (see Jewish scriptures)
    philosophical interpretation   18, 21

"seed of goodness"   22
self-love   4, 10, 25, 26, 27, 28, 29, 30, 31, 35, 40, 43, 45, 46, 47, 52, 64, 67, 85, 102
sensible beings   4, 135, 139
Sermon on the Mount   11, 114, 118, 130, 137
"servants of the church"   91
service of God, in religion   114–20
servile worship   124
Silber, John   30, 31, 45
sin
    guilty   37
    universality   36
    see also specific entries
"slavish faith"   99
    see also faith
"Son of God"   65, 70, 77, 91, 103
"Spirit of Christianity and Its Fate, The"   136, 137
spiritual despotism   3, 124, 125, 131
Stanglin, Keith D.   73n. 1
statutory religion   138, 139
    counterfeit service of God in   120–32
    see also religion
Stoics   61
supernatural faith see faith
supernaturalists   116
supernatural revelation see revelation
supersensible   3, 110, 115, 121
superstition   3, 55, 59, 91
    see also "pagan superstition"
Symbolism of Evil, The   139

temple service   124
Ten Commandments   106
thaumaturgy   55, 59
theistic miracles   83, 84, 126–7
    see also individual entries
theocracy   89, 106
theoretical cognition   110, 133

theoretical knowledge   102, 133, 134
Tofoa   47
tolerance, shared commitment to   2
traditional Christian theology   19, 75
  see also Christian theology
tradition(s)   3, 5, 9, 95
  Christian   57
  of critical thinking   60
  Protestant   75
Tree of Knowledge of Good and Evil   20, 52
Trinity   109, 110, 111
true visible church   91, 92, 94
  see also church

unconditional command, of moral law   4, 13, 14, 15, 27, 28, 29, 36, 47, 51, 73, 102, 112, 125, 137
  see also moral law(s)

universal religion *see* religion
universal rule   118–19
"unsocial sociability"   85, 86
Urbild   64, 91, 143

"vices of culture"   85
violence   1, 2, 108, 122
virtue   4, 10, 15, 36, 47, 56, 61, 69, 70, 76, 108, 112, 119, 122, 132, 134, 135, 136
visible church   90–2, 94, 95
  see also church

Wars of Religion   1
"What Does It Mean to Orient Oneself in Thinking?"   60, 142
Wille (will)   139
Wöllner, Johann Christoph   5, 6
Wood, Allen   85, 134
"works"   77–8
worship   94, 95, 109, 121, 123, 124, 130, 131

www.ingramcontent.com/pod-product-compliance
Ingram Content Group UK Ltd.
Pitfield, Milton Keynes, MK11 3LW, UK
UKHW020820240326
469204UK00019B/122